TOP NOTCH

English for Today's World

1

Maria Claudia Patino

Joan Saslow ■ Allen Ascher

With *Top Notch Pop Songs and Karaoke*
by Rob Morsberger

PEARSON
Longman

Top Notch: English for Today's World   1

Pearson Education, 10 Bank Street, White Plains, NY 10606

Editorial director: Pamela Fishman
Senior development editor: Peter Benson
Vice president, director of design and production: Rhea Banker
Director of electronic production: Aliza Greenblatt
Managing editor: Mike Kemper
Art director: Ann France
Senior manufacturing buyer: Dave Dickey
Photo research: Aerin Csigay
Digital layout specialist: Warren Fischbach
Text composition: Studio Montage
Text font: Palatino 11/13
Cover Photograph: "From Above," by Rhea Banker. Copyright © 2005 Rhea Banker.

4.3.2.1 CIP data was provided for the original edition

The Library of Congress has cataloged the ealier edition as follows:

Saslow, Joan M.
  Top notch : English for today's world. Student book. 1 / Joan Saslow, Allen Ascher.
      p. cm.
  1. English language--Textbooks for foreign speakers. 2. English language--Problems, exercises, etc. I. Ascher, Allen. II.
Title.
PE1128.S2757 2006
428.2'4--dc22   2003066101

ISBNs: 0-13-184035-5 (pbk. : alk. paper)
    0-13-174920-X (Student's Book with Take-Home Super CD-ROM)

Photo credits: All original photography by Michal Heron; page 4 (top left) Michael S. Yamashita/ Corbis, (top right) Peter Turnley/Corbis, (middle left) Jose Luis Pelaez, Inc./Corbis, (middle right) Ariel Skelley/Corbis; p. 5 (J. Groban) Robert Mora/Getty Images, (M. Streep) Mitchell Gerber/Corbis, (Y. Ming) AP/Wide World Photos; p. 8 Benjamin Rondel/Corbis; p. 9 (left) Tom Wagner/Corbis SABA, (right) Gary Brasch/Corbis; p. 22 (top) Dinodia Picture Agency, (bottom) Bassouls Sophie/Corbis Sygma; p. 23 (top) Salsatap.com, (bottom) Elizabeth Hansen, Adams/Hansen Photography; p. 28 (grandparents) Lindy Powers/Index Stock Imagery, (uncle, aunt, cousins) Getty Images, (parents) Ryan McVay/Getty Images, (mother-in-law) Ron Chapple/Getty Images, (father-in-law) James Darell/Getty Images, (sister-in-law, brother, nephew, niece) Royalty Free/Corbis, (sister) Cleve Bryant/PhotoEdit, (brother-in-law) Bill Cannon/Getty Images; p. 29 Rachel Epstein/PhotoEdit; p. 31 (middle) Lisette Le Bon/SuperStock, (bottom) Getty Images; p. 32 (chef) Gary Conner/Index Stock Imagery, (Sydney) David R. Frazier Photolibrary, Inc., (Bankok) Steve Vidler/estock Photography LLC; p. 33 (doctors) Jeff Isaac Greenberg/Photo Researchers, Inc., (girls with flowers) Myrleen Ferguson Cate/PhotoEdit, (shoe store) Jeff Greenberg/PhotoEdit; p. 36 (top) B. Kraft/Corbis, (bottom) Yang Liu/Corbis; p. 39 (tree) Alan Kearney/Getty Images, (Anne Douglas) Kevin Winter/Getty Images, (Kirk Douglas) Chris Pizzello, (Diana Dill) Scott Gries/Getty Images, (Diandra Douglas) Ralph Dominguez/Globe Photos, Inc., (Michael Douglas) Chris Pizzello, (Catherine Zeta-Jones) Sean Gallup/Getty Images, (Cameron Douglas) Scott Gries/Getty Images, (Dylan Douglas) Dave Parker/Globe Photos, Inc., (Carys Douglas) Chris Pizzello/WireImage; pp. 40, 46 (Communicator) Seiko Instruments USA, Inc., (woman) Image Source/SuperStock; p. 42 (laptop) Michael Newman/PhotEdit; p. 43 (TV) Ryan McVay/Getty Images, (laptop) Apple Computer, Inc., (PDA) Ryan McVay/Getty Images, (printer) Epson America, Inc., (cell phone) Nokia, (CD burner) Iomega Corporation; p. 44 (microwave) Anthony Meshkinyar/Getty Images, (coffee maker) Andy Crawford/Dorling Kindersley Media Library, (hair dryer) Slver Burdett Ginn, (fax) EyeWire Collection/Getty Images, (photocopier) Getty Images; p. 47 (alarm) Zhenjiang Sanwei Plastic & Electrical Appliances Co.,Ltd., (pen) photo courtesy of Sharper Image; p. 52 (Thai shrimp) Live Streeter/Patrick Mcleavy/Dorling Kindersley Media Library, (Mexican soup) Brian Hagiwara/PictureArts Corporation, (Tomato salad) Image Source/Picturequest, (chicken) Tom Vano/PictureQuest, (Brazilian steak) (Fried fish) David Murray and Jules Selmes/Dorling Kindersley Media Library, (Ice cream) (apple pie) (German chocolate cake) Francisco Cruz/SuperStock; p. 55 EyeWire Collection/Getty Images; p. 56 John A. Rizzo/Getty Images; p. 60 (Veggies) C Squared Studios/Getty Images, (track) Tom Carter/PhotoEdit, (pool) Pat Lanza/Bruce Coleman Inc., (golf) David Cannon/Dorling Kindersley Media Library, (tennis) R.W. Jones/Corbis; pp. 69, 74 (park) Rudi Von Briel/PhotoEdit, (gym) David Sacks/Getty Images, (athletic field) Sergio Piumatti; p. 72 Martell/Boston Herald/Corbis Sygma; p. 76 (men's boxers, bathrobe) Comstock Royalty Free Division, pp. 76, 79 (windbreaker) Gerald Lopez/Dorling Kindersley Media Library, (handbag) Steve Gorton/Dorling Kindersley Media Library, (belt) Richard Megna, Fundamental Photographs, (running shoes) Siede Preis/Getty Images; p. 84 (top) Henry Herholdt/Getty Images, (middle) Wolfgang Kaehler Photography, (bottom) Fridmar Damm/eStock Photography LLC.; p. 88 (Rome) Louis A. Goldman/Photo Researchers, Inc., (Venice) Karen McCunnall/eStock Photography LLC, (Disney) Ron Dahlquist/SuperStock, (Magic Kingdom) Len Kaufman, (Africa) Gregory G. Dimijam MD/Photo Researchers, Inc.; p. 90 PhotoLibrary.com and Mark E. Gibson/Corbis; p. 92 Larry Williams/Corbis; p. 93 (zoo) Lawrence Migdale/Pix, (baseball game) SuperStock, (movie) Andre Jenny/ ImageState, (museum) Bob Krist/eStock Photography LLC.; p. 94 (Bhutan) Pete Oxford/Robert Harding World Imagery, (Rio) Stephanie Maze/Woodfin Camp & Associates, (students) Royalty Free/Corbis, (Sea Mountain) Rob Lewine/Corbis; p. 100 Gary Conner/Index Stock Imagery; p. 101 (station) Jeffrey Blackman/Index Stock Imagery, (train) Steve Vidler/eStock Photography LLC; p. 102 (Puebla) Chris Sharp/D. Donne Bryant Stock Photography; p. 104 Hans Georg Roth/Corbis; p. 106 Andres Morya Hinojosa/Morya Photography; p. 108 (train) Jim Winkley/Corbis, (ship) Ron Chapple/Getty Images; p. 114 (background) David Young-Wolff/PhotoEdit; p. 115 (digital camera) Epson America, Inc., (camcorder) Sony Electronics Inc., (DVD player) George B. Diebold/Corbis & Tom Carter/PhotoEdit, (MP3) William Whitehurst/Corbis, (scanner) Churchill & Klehr/Pearson Education/PH College; p. 121 Getty Images.

Illustration credits: M. Teresa Aguilar, pp. 100, 103; Kenneth Batelman, pp. 21, 55, 80, 83, 88, 89, 102, 109, 110, 117 (middle); Pierre Berthiaume, pp. 106, 110; Rich Burlew, pp. 39, 64; John Ceballos, pp. 15, 27, 51, 63, 75, 87, 99, 111, 123; Lane DuPont, p. 82 (bottom); Scott Fray, pp. 3, 61; Steve Gardner, p. 112; (bottom); Marty Harris, p. 91 (middle); Brian Hughes, pp. 20, 22, 43, 45, 82 (top) 115; Andy Meyer, pp. 10, 14, 38, 46, 107, 108 (top); Sandy Nichols, pp. 26, 49, 58, 65, 66, 69, 70, 94, 104, 108 110, 119; Dusan Petricic, pp. 19, 57, 68, 96, 120; Rodico Prato, p. 16; Robert Saunders, pp. 31, 34, 90, 91 (top); Phil Scheuer, pp. 48, 116, 117 (top).

Printed in the United States of America
5 6 7 8 9 10–QWD–10 09 08 07

Contents

REFERENCE SECTION

Scope and Sequence OF CONTENT AND SKILLS

GRAMMAR BOOSTER

UNIT	Vocabulary*	Conversation Strategies	Grammar	
1 **Getting Acquainted** *Page 4*	• Titles • Occupations • Nationalities	• Use <u>As a matter of fact</u> to introduce surprising information • Begin responses with a question to clarify • Provide information beyond <u>Yes</u> or <u>No</u> when answering a question	• The verb <u>be</u>: <u>Yes</u> / <u>no</u> questions Contractions Information questions • Possessive nouns and adjectives	• Further explanation of usage and form: <u>be</u> • Further explanation of form: possessive adjectives
2 **Going Out** *Page 16* *Top Notch* Song: "Going Out"	• Entertainment events • Kinds of music • Locations and directions	• Use <u>Really?</u> to show enthusiasm • Use <u>I'd love to</u> to accept an invitation • Use <u>I'd love to, but...</u> or <u>Thanks, but...</u> to decline • Use <u>Excuse me</u> to approach a stranger	• The verb <u>be</u>: Questions with <u>When</u>, <u>What time</u>, and <u>Where</u> Contractions • Prepositions of time and place: <u>On, in, at</u>	• Further explanation of usage: prepositions of time and place
3 **Talking about Families** *Page 28*	• Family relationships • Ways to describe similarities and differences • Marital status and relationships	• Start answers with <u>Well</u> to give oneself time to think • Use <u>That's great!</u> to show enthusiasm • Ask follow-up questions to keep a conversation going • Initiate polite conversation with <u>So</u>	• The simple present tense: Statements <u>Yes</u> / <u>no</u> questions Information questions	• Further explanation of usage and form: the simple present tense
4 **Coping with Technology** *Page 40*	• Descriptive adjectives • Electronics • Ways to sympathize • Machines at home and at work • Machine features • Ways to state a complaint	• Use <u>How's it going?</u> and <u>Hey</u> to greet someone informally • Use word stress to clarify meaning • Use <u>What about...?</u> to make a suggestion • Use <u>Really?</u> to ask for confirmation • Use <u>Hello?</u> to answer the telephone	• The present continuous: for actions in progress and the future	• Spelling rules for the present participle • Further explanation of form: the present continuous
5 **Eating in, Eating out** *Page 52* *Top Notch* Song: "The World Café"	• Menu items • Categories of food • What to say to a waiter or waitress • Food and health	• Use <u>I think I'll have</u> to soften food orders • Use <u>Good idea!</u> to accept a suggestion enthusiastically	• Count and non-count nouns / <u>there is</u> and <u>there are</u> • <u>A</u>, <u>an</u>, <u>the</u>	• Categories of non-count nouns • Verb agreement: non-count nouns • Expressing quantities: non-count nouns • <u>How much</u> / <u>How many</u> • Spelling rules: plural nouns • <u>Some</u> / <u>any</u>

*In *Top Notch*, the term *vocabulary* refers to individual words, phrases, and expressions.

Speaking	Pronunciation	Listening	Reading	Writing
• Exchange personal information • Clarify and confirm information • Offer to introduce someone • Introduce someone • Shift to informality	• Rising and falling intonation for questions	• Conversations about people Task: listen for names, occupations, and nationalities	• Short introductions to people who travel for their jobs • Student descriptions	• Introduce a classmate • Introduce yourself
• Offer, accept, and decline invitations • Ask and answer questions about events • Ask for and give directions • Talk about music likes and dislikes	• Repetition to confirm information	• Invitations to events Task: identify the events and times • Phone calls to a box office Task: identify events, times, and ticket prices	• Newspaper entertainment listings • Arts festival website • People's descriptions of their musical tastes • Music survey	• Describe your own musical tastes
• Identify family relationships • Ask about and describe family members • Compare people • Discuss family size	• Blending sounds: <u>Does</u> + <u>he</u> / <u>Does</u> + <u>she</u>	• Descriptions of family members Task: listen for people's marital status or relationship • An interview about a brother Task: determine similarities and differences • Descriptions of families Task: determine size of family and number of children	• Article about different family sizes • Article comparing a brother and sister	• Compare two people in your own family • Compare two siblings in another family
• Ask for and make suggestions • Offer reasons for purchasing a product • Express frustration and offer sympathy • Describe features of machines • Complain when things don't work	• Rising and falling intonation for questions: review	• Complaints about machines Task: identify the machines • Radio advertisements Task: listen for adjectives that describe machines • Complaints to a hotel front desk Task: identify the problem and room number • Problems with machines Task: write the problem	• Ads from electronics catalogs	• Describe one of your own machines • Describe all the problems in a picture
• Discuss what to eat • Order, get the check, and pay for a meal • Describe your own diet • Discuss food and health choices	• Pronunciation of <u>the</u> before consonant and vowel sounds	• Conversations about food Task: listen for and classify food items • Conversations in a restaurant Task: predict a diner's next statement • Conversations while eating Task: determine the location of the conversation	• Menus • Nutrition website	• Describe a traditional food in your own country • Write a story based on a picture

Scope and Sequence OF CONTENT AND SKILLS

GRAMMAR BOOSTER

UNIT	Vocabulary	Conversation Strategies	Grammar	
6 **Staying in Shape** Page 64 *Top Notch* Song: "A Typical Day"	• Physical and everyday activities • Places for sports and games • Talking about health habits	• Use <u>Sorry, I can't</u> to decline regretfully • Provide an explanation for declining an invitation • Use <u>Actually</u> to introduce contrast	• <u>Can</u> and <u>have to</u> • The simple present tense and the present continuous • Frequency adverbs • Time expressions	• Further explanation of form: <u>can</u> / <u>have to</u> • Non-action verbs • Further explanation of usage and form: frequency adverbs / time expressions
7 **Finding Something to Wear** Page 76	• Categories of clothing • Clothing described as "pairs" • Types of clothing and shoes • Interior locations and directions • Describing clothes	• Use <u>Excuse me</u> to indicate that you need assistance in a store • Use <u>Excuse me?</u> when you don't understand or didn't hear	• Comparative adjectives • Object pronouns: as direct objects and in prepositional phrases	• Further explanation of spelling and usage: comparative adjectives • Further explanation of usage: direct and indirect objects
8 **Getting Away** Page 88 *Top Notch* Song: "My Dream Vacation"	• Types of vacations • Adjectives for travel conditions • Adjectives to describe vacations • Travel problems	• Use <u>actually</u> to acknowledge another's interest • Say <u>I'm fine</u> to decline assistance • After answering a question, ask <u>What about you?</u> to show reciprocal interest	• The past tense of <u>be</u> • The simple past tense: regular and irregular verbs	• Further explanation of usage and form: the past tense of <u>be</u> • Further explanation of usage and form: the simple past tense • Spelling rules: regular verbs in the simple past tense
9 **Taking Transportation** Page 100	• Tickets and trips • Travel services • Airline passenger information • Means of transportation • Transportation problems	• Say <u>Oh no</u> to indicate dismay • Say <u>Let me check</u> to buy time to find the answer to a question	• <u>Could</u> and <u>should</u> • <u>Be going to</u> for the future	• Further explanation of meaning: <u>can</u>, <u>should</u>, <u>could</u> • Explanation of form: modals • Comparison of ways to express the future
10 **Shopping Smart** Page 112 *Top Notch* Song: "Shopping for Souvenirs"	• Money and travel • Electronic products • Handicrafts • Talking about prices	• Use <u>can</u> to indicate willingness to bargain • Use demonstratives to clarify intention	• Superlative adjectives • <u>Too</u> and <u>enough</u>	• Contrasting the comparative and the superlative • Spelling rules for superlatives • Intensifiers <u>too</u>, <u>really</u>, and <u>very</u>

Speaking	Pronunciation	Listening	Reading	Writing
• Suggest and plan an activity • Provide an excuse • Ask about and describe daily routines • Discuss exercise and diet	• <u>Can</u> / <u>can't</u> • Third-person singular endings	• Conversations about immediate plans <u>Task</u>: identify destinations • Descriptions of exercise and diet routines <u>Task</u>: identify each person's health habits • Conversations about diet and exercise <u>Task</u>: complete the statement	• Graph showing calories burned by activity • Health survey • Article about Brooke Ellison's daily schedule	• Report about a classmate's typical day • Recount your own typical day
• Discuss where you shop • Ask a clerk for help • Shop and pay for clothes • Ask for and give directions within a building • Discuss culturally appropriate dress	• Contrastive stress for clarification	• Conversations about clothing needs <u>Task</u>: choose the clothing item • Directions in a store <u>Task</u>: mark the store departments • Conversations about clothes <u>Task</u>: determine the location of the conversation	• Clothing store website • Article about clothing tips for travelers • Personal dress code survey	• Give advice about clothing for visitors to your country • Plan clothing for a trip and explain reasons
• Greet someone arriving from a trip • Describe travel conditions • Talk about leisure activities • Discuss vacation preferences • Complain about travel problems	• Simple past-tense endings	• Descriptions of vacations <u>Task</u>: identify the vacation problems • Descriptions of travel experiences <u>Task</u>: choose the correct adjective	• Vacation ads • Travel agency brochure • Vacation survey • Student articles about vacations	• Describe a past vacation • Describe another person's vacation
• Discuss schedules and buy tickets • Ask for and give advice • Book travel services • Discuss travel plans • Describe transportation problems	• Intonation of alternatives	• Requests for travel services <u>Task</u>: identify the service requested • Airport announcements <u>Task</u>: listen for delays and cancellations • Conversations about transportation problems <u>Task</u>: complete the statement • Conversations about transportation <u>Task</u>: match the conversation with the picture	• Airport departure schedule • Travel survey • News clippings about transportation problems	• Recount transportation problems on a past trip • Imagine your next trip
• Ask for and give a recommendation • Discuss price range • Bargain for a lower price • Discuss tipping customs • Describe a shopping experience	• Rising intonation to clarify information	• Recommendations for electronic products <u>Task</u>: identify the product • Shopping stories <u>Task</u>: listen for products and prices • Conversations about electronics purchases <u>Task</u>: check satisfactory or not satisfactory to the customer	• Travel guide about money and shopping • Article about tipping customs • Tipping survey • Story about a shopping experience	• Narrate a true story about a shopping experience • Create a shopping guide for your city

Acknowledgments

Top Notch International Advisory Board

The authors gratefully acknowledge the substantive and formative contributions of the members of the International Advisory Board.

CHERYL BELL, Middlesex County College, Middlesex, New Jersey, USA • **ELMA CABAHUG**, City College of San Francisco, San Francisco, California, USA • **JO CARAGATA**, Mukogawa Women's University, Hyogo, Japan • **ANN CARTIER**, Palo Alto Adult School, Palo Alto, California, USA • **TERRENCE FELLNER**, Himeji Dokkyo University, Hyogo, Japan • **JOHN FUJIMORI**, Meiji Gakuin High School, Tokyo, Japan • **ARETA ULHANA GALAT**, Escola Superior de Estudos Empresariais e Informática, Curitiba, Brazil • **DOREEN M. GAYLORD**, Kanazawa Technical College, Ishikawa, Japan • **EMILY GEHRMAN**, Newton International College, Garden Grove, California, USA • **ANN-MARIE HADZIMA**, National Taiwan University, Taipei, Taiwan • **KAREN KYONG-AI PARK**, Seoul National University, Seoul, Korea • **ANA PATRICIA MARTÍNEZ VITE DIP. R.S.A.**, Universidad del Valle de México, Mexico City, Mexico • **MICHELLE ANN MERRITT**, Proulex/ Universidad de Guadalajara, Guadalajara, Mexico • **ADRIANNE P. OCHOA**, Georgia State University, Atlanta, Georgia, USA • **LOUIS PARDILLO**, Korea Herald English Institute, Seoul, Korea • **THELMA PERES**, Casa Thomas Jefferson, Brasilia, Brazil • **DIANNE RUGGIERO**, Broward Community College, Davie, Florida, USA • **KEN SCHMIDT**, Tohoku Fukushi University, Sendai, Japan • **ALISA A. TAKEUCHI**, Garden Grove Adult Education, Garden Grove, California, USA • **JOSEPHINE TAYLOR**, Centro Colombo Americano, Bogotá, Colombia • **PATRICIA VECIÑO**, Instituto Cultural Argentino Norteamericano, Buenos Aires, Argentina • **FRANCES WESTBROOK**, AUA Language Center, Bangkok, Thailand

Reviewers and Piloters

Many thanks also to the reviewers and piloters all over the world who reviewed *Top Notch* in its final form.

G. Julian Abaqueta, Huachiew Chalermprakiet University, Samutprakarn, Thailand • **David Aline**, Kanagawa University, Kanagawa, Japan • **Marcia Alves**, Centro Cultural Brasil Estados Unidos, Franca, Brazil • **Yousef Al-Yacoub**, Qatar Petroleum, Doha, Qatar • **Maristela Barbosa Silveira e Silva**, Instituto Cultural Brasil-Estados Unidos, Manaus, Brazil • **Beth Bartlett**, Centro Colombo Americano, Cali, Colombia • **Carla Battigelli**, University of Zulia, Maracaibo, Venezuela • **Claudia Bautista**, C.B.C., Caracas, Venezuela • **Rob Bell**, Shumei Yachiyo High School, Chiba, Japan • **Dr. Maher Ben Moussa**, Sharjah University, Sharjah, United Arab Emirates • **Elaine Cantor**, Englewood Senior High School, Jacksonville, Florida, USA • **María Aparecida Capellari**, SENAC, São Paulo, Brazil • **Eunice Carrillo Ramos**, Colegio Durango, Naucalpan, Mexico • **Janette Carvalhinho de Oliveira**, Centro de Linguas (UFES), Vitória, Brazil • **María Amelia Carvalho Fonseca**, Centro Cultural Brasil-Estados Unidos, Belém, Brazil • **Audy Castañeda**, Instituto Pedagógico de Caracas, Caracas, Venezuela • **Ching-Fen Chang**, National Chiao Tung University, Hsinchu, Taiwan • **Ying-Yu Chen**, Chinese Culture University, Taipei, Taiwan • **Joyce Chin**, The Language Training and Testing Center, Taipei, Taiwan • **Eun Cho**, Pagoda Language School, Seoul, Korea • **Hyungzung Cho**, MBC Language Institute, Seoul, Korea • **Dong Sua Choi**, MBC Language Institute, Seoul, Korea • **Jeong Mi Choi**, Freelancer, Seoul, Korea • **Peter Chun**, Pagoda Language School, Seoul, Korea • **Eduardo Corbo**, Legacy ELT, Salto, Uruguay • **Marie Cosgrove**, Surugadai University, Saitama, Japan • **María Antonieta Covarrubias Souza**, Centro Escolar Akela, Mexico City, Mexico • **Katy Cox**, Casa Thomas Jefferson, Brasilia, Brazil • **Michael Donovan**, Gakushuin University, Tokyo, Japan • **Stewart Dorward**, Shumei Eiko High School, Saitama, Japan • **Ney Eric Espina**, Centro Venezolano Americano del Zulia, Maracaibo, Venezuela • **Edith Espino**, Centro Especializado de Lenguas - Universidad Tecnológica de Panamá, El Dorado, Panama • **Allen P. Fermon**, Instituto Brasil-Estados Unidos, Ceará, Brazil • **Simão Ferreira Banha**, Phil Young's English School, Curitiba, Brazil • **María Elena Flores Lara**, Colegio Mercedes, Mexico City, Mexico • **Valesca Fróis Nassif**, Associação Cultural Brasil-Estados Unidos, Salvador, Brazil • **José Fuentes**, Empire Language Consulting, Caracas, Venezuela • **José Luis Guerrero**, Colegio Cristóbal Colón, Mexico City, Mexico • **Claudia Patricia Gutiérrez**, Centro Colombo Americano, Cali, Colombia • **Valerie Hansford**, Asia University, Tokyo, Japan • **Gene Hardstark**, Dotkyo University, Saitama, Japan • **Maiko Hata**, Kansai University, Osaka, Japan • **Susan Elizabeth Haydock Miranda de Araujo**, Centro Cultural Brasil Estados Unidos, Belém, Brazil • **Gabriela Herrera**, Fundametal, Valencia, Venezuela • **Sandy Ho**, GEOS International, New York, New York, USA • **Yuri Hosoda**, Showa Women's University, Tokyo, Japan • **Hsiao-I Hou**, Shu-Te University, Kaohsiung County, Taiwan • **Kuei-ping Hsu**, National Tsing Hua University, Hsinchu, Taiwan • **Chia-yu Huang**, National Tsing Hua University, Hsinchu, Taiwan • **Caroline C. Hwang**, National Taipei University of Science and Technology, Taipei, Taiwan • **Diana Jones**, Angloamericano, Mexico City, Mexico • **Eunjeong Kim**, Freelancer, Seoul, Korea • **Julian Charles King**, Qatar Petroleum, Doha, Qatar • **Bruce Lee**, CIE: Foreign Language Institute, Seoul, Korea • **Myunghee Lee**, MBC Language Institute, Seoul, Korea • **Naidnapa Leoprasertkul**, Language Development Center, Mahasarakham University, Mahasarakham, Thailand • **Eleanor S. Leu**, Souchow University, Taipei, Taiwan • **Eliza Liu**, Chinese Culture University, Taipei, Taiwan • **Carlos Lizárraga**, Angloamericano, Mexico City, Mexico • **Philippe Loussarevian**, Keio University Shonan Fujisawa High School, Kanagawa, Japan • **Jonathan Lynch**, Azabu University, Tokyo, Japan • **Thomas Mach**, Konan University, Hyogo, Japan • **Lilian Mandel Civatti**, Associação Cultural Brasil-Estados Unidos, Salvador, Brazil • **Hakan Mansuroglu**, Zoni Language Center, West New York, New Jersey, USA • **Martha McGaughey**, Language Training Institute, Englewood Cliffs, New Jersey, USA • **David Mendoza Plascencia**, Instituto Internacional de Idiomas, Naucalpan, Mexico • **Theresa Mezo**, Interamerican University, Río Piedras, Puerto Rico • **Luz Adriana Montenegro Silva**, Colegio CAFAM, Bogotá, Colombia • **Magali de Moraes Menti**, Instituto Lingua, Porto Alegre, Brazil • **Massoud Moslehpour**, The Overseas Chinese Institute of Technology, Taichung, Taiwan • **Jennifer Nam**, IKE, Seoul, Korea • **Marcos Norelle F. Victor**, Instituto Brasil-Estados Unidos, Ceará, Brazil • **Luz María Olvera**, Instituto Juventud del Estado de México, Naucalpan, Mexico • **Roxana Orrego Ramírez**, Universidad Diego Portales, Santiago, Chile • **Ming-Jong Pan**, National Central University, Jhongli City, Taiwan • **Sandy Park**, Topia Language School, Seoul, Korea • **Patrícia Elizabeth Peres Martins**, Instituto Brasil-Estados Unidos, Rio de Janeiro, Brazil • **Rodrigo Peza**, Passport Language Centers, Bogotá, Colombia • **William Porter**, Osaka Institute of Technology, Osaka, Japan • **Caleb Prichard**, Kwansei Gakuin University, Hyogo, Japan • **Mirna Quintero**, Instituto Pedagógico de Caracas, Caracas, Venezuela • **Roberto Rabbini**, Seigakuin University, Saitama, Japan • **Terri Rapoport**, Berkeley College, White Plains, New York, USA • **Yvette Rieser**, Centro Electrónico de Idiomas, Maracaibo, Venezuela • **Orlando Rodríguez**, New English Teaching School, Paysandu, Uruguay • **Mayra Rosario**, Pontificia Universidad Católica Madre y Maestra, Santiago, Dominican Republic • **Peter Scout**, Sakura no Seibo Junior College, Fukushima, Japan • **Jungyeon Shim**, EG School, Seoul, Korea • **Keum Ok Song**, MBC Language Institute, Seoul, Korea • **Assistant Professor Dr. Reongrudee Soonthornmanee**, Chulalongkorn University Language Institute, Bangkok, Thailand • **Claudia Stanisclause**, The Language College, Maracay, Venezuela • **Tom Suh**, The Princeton Review, Seoul, Korea • **Phiphawin Suphawat**, KhonKaen University, KhonKaen, Thailand • **Craig Sweet**, Poole Gakuin Junior and Senior High Schools, Osaka, Japan • **Yi-nien Josephine Twu**, National Tsing Hua University, Hsinchu, Taiwan • **Maria Christina Uchôa Close**, Instituto Cultural Brasil-Estados Unidos, São José dos Campos, Brazil • **Luz Vanegas Lopera**, Lexicom The Place For Learning English, Medellín, Colombia • **Julieta Vasconcelos García**, Centro Escolar del Lago, A.C., Mexico City, Mexico • **Carol Vaughan**, Kanto Kokusai High School, Tokyo, Japan • **Patricia Celia Veciño**, Instituto Cultural Argentino Norteamericano, Buenos Aires, Argentina • **Isabela Villas Boas**, Casa Thomas Jefferson, Brasilia, Brazil • **Iole Vitti**, Peanuts English School, Poços de Caldas, Brazil • **Gabi Witthaus**, Qatar Petroleum, Doha, Qatar • **Yi-Ling Wu**, Shih Chien University, Taipei, Taiwan • **Chad Wynne**, Osaka Keizai University, Osaka, Japan • **Belkis Yanes**, Freelance Instructor, Caracas, Venezuela • **I-Chieh Yang**, Chung-kuo Institute of Technology, Taipei, Taiwan • **Emil Ysona**, Instituto Cultural Dominico-Americano, Santo Domingo, Dominican Republic • **Chi-fang Yu**, Soo Chow University, Taipei, Taiwan, • **Shigeki Yusa**, Sendai Shirayuri Women's College, Sendai, Japan

To the Teacher

What is *Top Notch*?

- *Top Notch* is a six-level communicative English course for adults and young adults, with two beginning entry levels.
- *Top Notch* prepares students to interact successfully and confidently with both native and non-native speakers of English.
- *Top Notch* demonstrably brings students to a "Top Notch" level of communicative competence.

Key Elements of the *Top Notch* Instructional Design

Concise two-page lessons

Each easy-to-teach two-page lesson is designed for one class session and begins with a clearly stated communication goal and ends with controlled or free communication practice. Each lesson provides vocabulary, grammar, and social language contextualized in all four skills, keeping the pace of a class session lively and varied.

Daily confirmation of progress

Adult and young adult students need to observe and confirm their own progress. In *Top Notch*, students conclude each class session with a controlled or free practice activity that demonstrates their ability to use new vocabulary, grammar, and social language. This motivates and keeps students eager to continue their study of English and builds their pride in being able to speak accurately, fluently, and authentically.

Real language

Carefully exposing students to authentic, natural English, both receptively and productively, is a necessary component of building understanding and expression. All conversation models feature the language people really use; nowhere to be found is "textbook English" written merely to exemplify grammar.

Practical content

In addition to classic topical vocabulary, grammar, and conversation, *Top Notch* includes systematic practice of highly practical language, such as: how to ask for a restaurant check, how to ask whether the tip is included in the bill, how to complain when the air-conditioning in a hotel room doesn't work, how to bargain for a lower price—usable language today's students want and need.

Memorable model conversations

Effective language instruction must make language memorable. The full range of social and functional communicative needs is presented through practical model conversations that are intensively practiced and manipulated, first within a guided model and then in freer and more personalized formats.

High-impact vocabulary syllabus

In order to ensure students' solid acquisition of vocabulary essential for communication, *Top Notch* contains explicit presentation, practice, and systematic extended recycling of words, collocations, and expressions appropriate at each level of study. The extensive captioned illustrations, photos, definitions, examples, and contextualized sentences remove doubts about meaning and provide a permanent in-book reference for student test preparation. An added benefit is that teachers don't have to search for pictures to bring to class and don't have to resort to translating vocabulary into the students' native language.

Learner-supportive grammar

Grammar is approached explicitly and cognitively, through form, meaning, and use—both within the Student's Book units and in a bound-in Grammar Booster. Charts provide examples and paradigms enhanced by simple usage notes at students' level of comprehension. This takes the guesswork out of meaning, makes lesson preparation easier for teachers, and provides students with comprehensible charts for permanent reference and test preparation. All presentations of grammar are followed by exercises to ensure adequate practice.

English as an international language

Top Notch prepares students for interaction with both native and non-native speakers of English, both linguistically and culturally. English is treated as an international language, rather than the language of a particular country or region. In addition, *Top Notch* helps students develop a cultural fluency by creating an awareness of the varied rules across cultures for: politeness, greetings and introductions, appropriateness of dress in different settings, conversation do's and taboos, table manners, and other similar issues.

Two beginning-level texts

Beginning students can be placed either in *Top Notch 1* or *Top Notch Fundamentals*, depending on ability and background. Even absolute beginners can start with confidence in *Top Notch Fundamentals*. False beginners can begin with *Top Notch 1*. The *Top Notch Placement Test* clarifies the best placement within the series.

Estimated teaching time

Each level of *Top Notch* is designed for 60 to 90 instructional hours and contains a full range of supplementary components and enrichment devices to tailor the course to individual needs.

Components of *Top Notch 1*

Student's Book with Take-Home Super CD-ROM

The Super CD-ROM includes a variety of exciting interactive activities: Speaking Practice, Interactive Workbook, Games and Puzzles, and *Top Notch Pop* Karaoke. The disk can also be played on an audio CD player to listen to the Conversation Models and the five *Top Notch Pop* songs.

Teacher's Edition and Lesson Planner

Complete yet concise lesson plans are provided for each class. Corpus notes provide essential information from the *Longman Spoken American Corpus* and the *Longman Learner's Corpus*. In addition, a free Teacher's Resource Disk offers the following printable extension activities to personalize your teaching style:

- Grammar self-checks
- *Top Notch Pop* song activities
- Writing process worksheets
- Learning strategies
- Pronunciation activities and supplements
- Extra reading comprehension activities
- Vocabulary cards and cumulative vocabulary activities
- Graphic organizers
- Pair work cards

Copy & Go: Ready-made Interactive Activities for Busy Teachers

Interactive games, puzzles, and other practice activities in convenient photocopiable form

support the Student's Book content and provide a welcome change of pace.

Complete Classroom Audio Program

The audio program contains listening comprehension activities, rhythm and intonation practice, and targeted pronunciation activities that focus on accurate and comprehensible pronunciation.

Because *Top Notch* prepares students for international communication, a variety of native and non-native speakers are included to ready students for the world outside the classroom. The audio program also includes the five *Top Notch Pop* songs in standard and karaoke form.

Workbook

A tightly linked illustrated Workbook contains exercises that provide additional practice and reinforcement of language concepts and skills from *Top Notch* and its Grammar Booster.

Complete Assessment Package with *ExamView®* Software

Ten easy-to-administer and easy-to-score unit achievement tests assess listening, vocabulary, grammar, social language, reading, and writing. Two review tests, one mid-book and one end-of-book, provide additional cumulative assessment. Two speaking tests assess progress in speaking. In addition to the photocopiable achievement tests, *ExamView®* software enables teachers to tailor-make tests to best meet their needs by combining items in any way they wish.

Top Notch TV

A lively and entertaining video offers a TV-style situation comedy that reintroduces language from each *Top Notch* unit, plus authentic unrehearsed interviews with English speakers from around the world and authentic karaoke. Packaged with the video are activity worksheets and a booklet with teaching suggestions and complete video scripts.

Companion Website

A Companion Website at www.longman.com/topnotch provides numerous additional resources for students and teachers. This no-cost, high-benefit feature includes opportunities for further practice of language and content from the *Top Notch* Student's Book.

Welcome to Top Notch!

About the Authors

Joan Saslow

Joan Saslow has taught English as a Foreign Language and English as a Second Language to adults and young adults in both South America and the United States. She taught English and French at the Binational Centers of Valparaíso and Viña del Mar, Chile, and the Catholic University of Valparaíso. In the United States, Ms. Saslow taught English as a Foreign Language to Japanese university students at Marymount College and to international students in Westchester Community College's intensive English program as well as workplace English at the General Motors auto assembly plant in Tarrytown, NY.

Ms. Saslow is the series director of Longman's popular five-level adult series *True Colors: An EFL Course for Real Communication* and of *True Voices*, a five-level video course. She is author of *Ready to Go: Language, Lifeskills, and Civics*, a four-level adult ESL series; *Workplace Plus*, a vocational English series; and of *Literacy Plus*, a two-level series that teaches literacy, English, and culture to adult pre-literate students. She is also author of *English in Context: Reading Comprehension for Science and Technology*, a three-level series for English for special purposes. In addition, Ms. Saslow has been an author, an editor of language teaching materials, a teacher-trainer, and a frequent speaker at gatherings of EFL and ESL teachers for over thirty years.

Allen Ascher

Allen Ascher has been a teacher and teacher-trainer in both China and the United States, as well as an administrator and a publisher. Mr. Ascher specialized in teaching listening and speaking to students at the Beijing Second Foreign Language Institute, to hotel workers at a major international hotel in China, and to Japanese students from Chubu University studying English at Ohio University. In New York, Mr. Ascher taught students of all language backgrounds and abilities at the City University of New York, and he trained teachers in the TESOL Certificate Program at the New School. He was also the academic director of the International English Language Institute at Hunter College.

Mr. Ascher has provided lively workshops for EFL teachers throughout Asia, Latin America, Europe, and the Middle East. He is author of the popular *Think about Editing: A Grammar Editing Guide for ESL Writers*. As a publisher, Mr. Ascher played a key role in the creation of some of the most widely used materials for adults, including: *True Colors, NorthStar, Focus on Grammar, Global Links*, and *Ready to Go*. Mr. Ascher has an M.A. in Applied Linguistics from Ohio University.

Welcome to *Top Notch!*

A 🎧 **Read and listen.** Then listen again and repeat in the pauses.

Hello. My name's Peter.

Hi. I'm Alexandra. But everyone calls me Alex.

🎧 **More greetings**
Good morning.
Good afternoon.
Good evening.

1. Introduce yourself.

What do you do?

I'm a student. And you?

I'm a student, too.

2. Tell someone what you do.

Alex, this is Emily. Emily, this is Alex.

Nice to meet you, Alex.

Nice to meet you, too.

3. Introduce someone.

Well, it was nice meeting you.

See you later.

Bye.

🎧 **More ways to say good-bye**
Good-bye.
Take it easy.
Take care.
Good night.

4. Say good-bye.

B **GROUP WORK.**
Get to know your classmates.

Introduce someone to your class.

C 🎧 **Read and listen. Then listen again and repeat in the pauses.**

1. What's this called in English? — A stapler. — A stapler? — Yes. That's right.

2. What's your last name, please? — Choi. — I'm sorry. Could you repeat that? — Sure. It's Choi.

3. How do you say your last name? — Yuan. — Yuan? Thanks.

4. How do you spell your first name? — G-U-Y. — Thank you.

D 🎧 **Listen to the conversations. Then listen again and write the names.**

1. _____   _____
   first name   last name

2. _____   _____
   first name   last name

E **PAIR WORK.** What's this called in English? Use your dictionary.

1. _____   2. _____   3. _____   4. _____

UNIT GOALS

1 Get to know someone
2 Offer to introduce someone
3 Talk about people
4 Interview a classmate

A **TOPIC PREVIEW.** Why are <u>you</u> studying English?

☐ for business

☐ for travel

☐ for study

☐ to get to know people who don't speak my language

B Enroll in *Top Notch*.

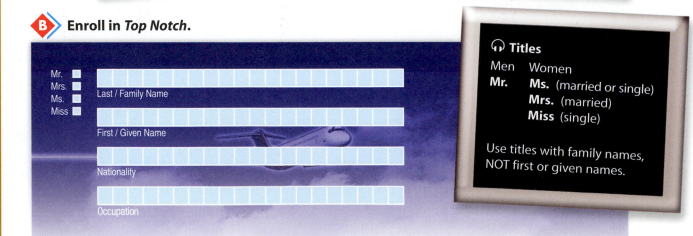

Mr. ☐
Mrs. ☐
Ms. ☐
Miss ☐

Last / Family Name

First / Given Name

Nationality

Occupation

🎧 **Titles**

Men	Women	
Mr.	**Ms.**	(married or single)
	Mrs.	(married)
	Miss	(single)

Use titles with family names, NOT first or given names.

C 🎧 **SOUND BITES.** Read along silently as you listen to a natural conversation.

DIANA: Mom, this is my teacher, Mr. Mills.

MRS. DARE: Nice to meet you, Mr. Mills.

MR. MILLS: Please call me Tom.

MR. MILLS: Let me introduce you to my wife, Carol.... Carol, Mrs. Dare and her daughter, Diana.

MRS. MILLS: Nice to meet you both.

D Complete each sentence.

1. Mrs. Dare calls Diana's teacher _____.
   a. Mr. Mills   **b.** Tom   **c.** Mr. Tom

2. Mr. Mills calls his wife _____.
   a. Carol   **b.** Mrs. Mills   **c.** Ms. Carol

3. Mr. Mills calls his student _____.
   a. Ms. Dare   **b.** Diana   **c.** Miss Dare

WHAT ABOUT **YOU?**

Complete your response to each person.

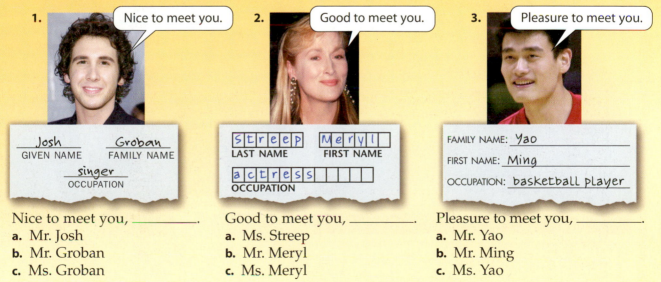

1. *Nice to meet you.*

Josh — GIVEN NAME Groban — FAMILY NAME
singer — OCCUPATION

Nice to meet you, _____.
a. Mr. Josh
b. Mr. Groban
c. Ms. Groban

2. *Good to meet you.*

Streep — LAST NAME Meryl — FIRST NAME
actress — OCCUPATION

Good to meet you, _____.
a. Ms. Streep
b. Mr. Meryl
c. Ms. Meryl

3. *Pleasure to meet you.*

FAMILY NAME: Yao
FIRST NAME: Ming
OCCUPATION: basketball player

Pleasure to meet you, _____.
a. Mr. Yao
b. Mr. Ming
c. Ms. Yao

1 Get to Know Someone

🎧 CONVERSATION MODEL Read and listen.

A: Are you Bill?
B: No, I'm David. That's Bill over there.
A: Well, I'm Stacey. It's nice to meet you, David.
B: You, too.
A: Are you a student here?
B: As a matter of fact, I am.

🎧 **Rhythm and intonation practice**

A **GRAMMAR.** Yes / no questions and short answers with the verb be

Are you a student?	Yes, I am.	No, I'm not.
Is he married?	Yes, he is.	No, he isn't. [No, he's not.]
Is Claire from the U.S.?	Yes, she is.	No, she isn't. [No, she's not.]
Are you in my class?	Yes, we are.	No, we aren't. [No, we're not.]
Are they Canadian?	Yes, they are.	No, they aren't. [No, they're not.]
Are your friends here?	Yes, they are.	No, they aren't. [No, they're not.]

Contractions
I'm = I am
you're = you are
he's = he is
she's = she is
we're = we are
they're = they are

GRAMMAR BOOSTER

PAGE G1
For more ...

B Complete the questions and answers. Use contractions when possible.

_____ from China?
1.

Yes, as a matter of fact,
_____ .
2.

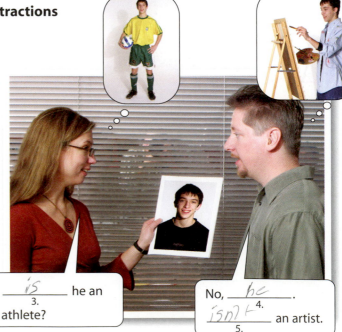

_is_ he an
3.
athlete?

No, _he_ .
4.
isn't an artist.
5.

Oh, those are the new students. _____ 6. from Canada?

No, _____ 7. . I think _____ 8. from the U.K.

Hello. _____ 9. Nancy and Ron?

No, _____ 10. . I'm Jake and this is Patty.

C **PAIR WORK.** Write questions for your partner. Then exchange questions. Write answers to your partner's questions.

Are you from São Paulo?

No, I'm not. I'm from Santos.

CONVERSATION PAIR WORK

Write all your classmates' names on the chalkboard. Then get to know your classmates. Use the guide, or create a new conversation.

A: Are you _____?

B: _____.

A: Well, I'm _____. It's nice to meet you, _____.

B: _____ ...

Continue the conversation in your own way.

CONTROLLED PRACTICE

2 ► *Offer to Introduce Someone*

🎧 **CONVERSATION** **MODEL** **Read and listen.**

A: Who's that?

B: Over there? Her name's Kate. Come. I'll introduce you.

• • •

B: Lauren, I'd like you to meet Kate.

A: Nice to meet you, Kate.

C: Nice to meet you, too.

🎧 **Rhythm and intonation practice**

A ◆ **GRAMMAR.** **Information questions with be**

Who's that?	That's Park Su.
Who are they?	They're my classmates.
Where's he from?	He's from Tokyo.
What's your occupation?	I'm a student.
How old are they?	He's sixteen and his brother is ten.
What's your nickname?	Everyone calls me Susie.
What are their names?	Costas and Ahmed.
What's his e-mail address?	ted@kr.com [say "ted at k r dot com"]

Possessive nouns
the **teacher's** name
Peter's address

Possessive adjectives
I = **my**   it = **its**
you = **your**   we = **our**
he = **his**   they = **their**
she = **her**

Contractions
Who's = Who is
What's = What is
Where's = Where is
That's = That is

GRAMMAR BOOSTER

PAGE G2
For more . . .

B ◆ **Complete the conversations.**
Use contractions when possible.

1. **A:** _____ that over there?
   B: Oh, that _____ Erol.
      He _____ from Turkey.
   A: _____ is he? He looks
      very young.
   B: I think he _____ twenty-five.

Istanbul, Turkey

2. A: _____ that your new neighbor?

   B: Yeah. _____ name _____ Roberta.

   A: _____ she from?

   B: Costa Rica.

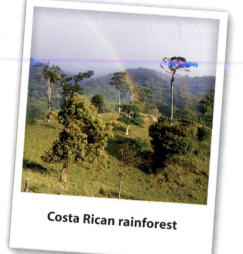

Costa Rican rainforest

Mieko and Rika

3. A: _____ they?

   B: Oh, _____ my classmates.

   A: _____ their names?

   B: That _____ Mieko on the left, and that _____ Rika on the right.

C ▷ PAIR WORK. Write questions for your partner. Then exchange questions. Answer your partner's questions.

> What's your father's name?

> His name is Paul.

D ▷ 🎧 PRONUNCIATION. Intonation. Use rising intonation in <u>yes</u> / <u>no</u> questions. Use falling intonation in information questions. Listen. Then listen again and repeat.

1. Is she French?
2. Who's that?
3. Are they married?
4. Where are they from?

CONVERSATION PAIR WORK

Offer to introduce your partner to other classmates. Use the guide, or create a new conversation.

A: Who's that?
B: Over there? _____ name's _____.
  Come. I'll introduce you.
  • • •
B: _____, I'd like you to meet _____.
A: _____ …

Continue the conversation in your <u>own</u> way.

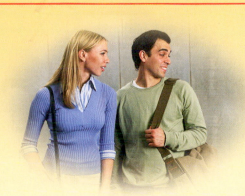

CONTROLLED PRACTICE

3 Talk about People

A 🎧 **VOCABULARY.** Some occupations. Listen and practice.

a computer programmer

a photographer

an interpreter

a musician

a manager

a chef

a salesperson

a flight attendant

a graphic designer

a pilot

B 🎧 **LISTENING COMPREHENSION.** Listen to the conversations about the people. Then listen again. Write the occupation and the nationality.

1. Fumiko Ito
graphic designer
Japanese

2. Lee Hyuk
_____
_____

3. Ilhan Ramic
_____
_____

4. Ana Gutierrez
_____
_____

NATIONALITIES

American

Turkish

Ecuadorian

Argentinean

Japanese

Spanish

Korean

Colombian

Partner A: Look at the top of the page.
Partner B: Look at the bottom of the page.
Ask questions and write the missing information.

PARTNER A

Name: Paul Melin
Occupation: Chef
Nationality: _____
Age: 43
E-mail address:
_____

Name: _____
Occupation: Photographer
Nationality: _____
Age: 36
E-mail address:
_____

Name: Chisoto Nakamura
Occupation: _____
Nationality: Japanese
Age: _____
E-mail address:
nakamurac@genki.com.jp

Name: Georges Hayek
Occupation: _____
Nationality: Lebanese
Age: _____
E-mail address:
hayek1435@lebworld.com

PARTNER B

Name: _____
Occupation: Interpreter
Nationality: _____
Age: 57
E-mail address: _____

Name: Chisoto Nakamura
Occupation: Musician
Nationality: _____
Age: 24
E-mail address: _____

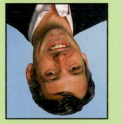

Name: Helena Da Silva
Occupation: _____
Nationality: Brazilian
Age: _____
E-mail address:
dasilva.helena@brasnet.com

Name: Paul Melin
Occupation: _____
Nationality: Canadian
Age: _____
E-mail address:
pmelin678@interlink.com

FREE PRACTICE

11

4 Interview a Classmate

A **READING WARM-UP.** Do you know people who travel a lot for their jobs? Where? What are their occupations?

B 🎧 **READING.** *Top Notch* interviewed people who travel for their jobs. Read about them.

CRISTINA PETRIZZI

Meet Maria Cristina Petrizzi S. Ferreira, 38, an interpreter and translator from Brazil. She works for some well-known Brazilian and international companies. Ms. Petrizzi lives in São Paulo with her husband, Roberto, and their daughter, Natalia. But her hometown is Santos, a town on the coast. "My work is great because I travel and get to know lots of people."

HIDETAKA KAMIMURA

This is Dr. Hidetaka Kamimura and his family. Dr. Kamimura is a manager in a pharmaceutical company. He was born in Shizuoka, in central Japan, in 1951. Today he lives in Tokyo with his wife, Yumi, and their three children. "I travel overseas for my job several times a year," he says. "But I really like to travel with my family."

ARLYS DOCKENDORFF

Meet Arlys Dockendorff, 52, a photographer. Ms. Dockendorff lives near New York City, but she comes from the state of Iowa in the center of the United States. She takes photographs around the world. "I like to photograph interesting people," she says. "Musicians, artists, children, old people." You can see her photographs of Tibet on the Internet at www.echinaart.com.

SOURCE: authentic *Top Notch* interviews

C Read about the people again. Complete the chart. Fill in each person's occupation, age, city, and hometown.

	Occupation	Age	Lives in . . .	Comes from . . .
Ms. Petrizzi				
Dr. Kamimura				
Ms. Dockendorff				

STEP 1. **Read the articles students wrote to introduce their classmates.**

This is Kyoko Hirano. She is an international marketing manager. She is from Tokyo, Japan. Ms. Hirano is 26 years old. She lives near New York with her sister, Motoko.

Kyoko Hirano

Arturo Paz

Meet Arturo Paz. What's his occupation? Arturo is a businessman. He lives in Caracas, Venezuela. He is 40 years old and married. His wife, Margarita, is an opera singer.

STEP 2. **PAIR WORK.** **Interview a classmate. Write his or her personal information on the notepad.**

Name:

Nickname:

Occupation:

Hometown:

Age:

Other:

STEP 3. **WRITING.** **Write a short article about your classmate.**

Francisco is my partner. He's a bank manager. His nickname is

A 🎧 **LISTENING COMPREHENSION.** Listen to the conversations at an international conference. Listen again and write each person's occupation and country or hometown.

	Occupation	From ...
1. Bill Anderson		
2. Penny Latulippe		
3. Mike Johnson		
4. Margo Brenner		

Australia
Scotland
Vancouver
the U.S.
San Diego
Peru

B **Look at the pictures below. Write the occupations.**

1. A _____ works in a restaurant.
2. A _____ works in an office.
3. A _____ works on an airplane.
4. A _____ works in a store.
5. A _____ works in a school.

1.　　　　　2.　　　　　3.　　　　　4.　　　　　5.

C **Complete each conversation in your own way.**

1. "Are you Pat?"
   YOU _____.

2. "What's your name?"
   YOU _____.

3. "Are you a new student?"
   YOU _____.

4. **YOU** _____?
   "I'm from Paraguay."

5. **YOU** _____?
   "I'm a musician."

6. **YOU** _____.
   "Nice to meet you, too."

D **WRITING.** Write a paragraph about yourself. Use the questions as a guide.

- What's your first and last name?
- What's your nickname?
- How old are you?
- What's your hometown?
- What's your occupation?

TOP NOTCH PROJECT
Create a class newsletter with photos to introduce your classmates.

TOP NOTCH WEBSITE
For Unit 1 online activities, visit the *Top Notch* Companion Website at www.longman.com/topnotch.

- **Vocabulary.** Look at the people and guess the occupations.

- **Social language.** Create conversations for the people.

  A: Are you _____?   A: This is _____.
  B: _____.   B: _____.

- **Grammar.** Ask and answer questions about the people.

GATE 6

MS. SMITH

XML
JAVA

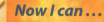 **Now I can...**

☐ get to know someone.
☐ offer to introduce someone.
☐ talk about people.
☐ interview a classmate.

UNIT GOALS

1 Accept or decline an invitation
2 Ask for and give directions
3 Make plans to see an event
4 Talk about musical tastes

A **TOPIC PREVIEW.** Look at the newspaper entertainment page. Choose a concert. Circle the date of the concert on the calendar. Circle the location on the map.

THURSDAY, JUNE 19 *THE GARNET CITY GAZETTE*

WEEKEND LISTINGS

LATIN
Pilar Montenegro. Latin dance-pop music from Mexico. 8 p.m. June 22. Grant Park Band Shell, Grant Park (between First and Second Ave). $25 in advance/$35 on the day of show. Tickets: 622-4408.

CLASSICAL
Kyung-wha Chung. Korean violinist performs Debussy's Sonata for Violin and Piano. With pianist Radu Lupu. 7:15 p.m. June 20. Symphony Hall, 500 First Ave. (across from Grant Park). Tickets: $35–$75. Box office: 622-6000.

ROCK
Guitar Wolf. Japanese Rock Showcase. 10:30 p.m. June 21. Maxwell's, corner of Second Ave. and Market St. Tickets: $8 in advance/ $10 at the door. Box office: 622-1736.

JAZZ
Sergio Mendes. The king of Bossa Nova jazz returns with his group, Brasil. 8:00 and 11:30 p.m. June 21. The Downbeat, 303 First Ave. Call for ticket prices: 622-1209.

Downtown Garnet City

SECOND AVE.
Band Shell
Grant Park
FIRST AVE.
Symphony Hall
GRAND ST.
Maxwell's
PARK ST.
The Downbeat
MARKET ST.

June

SUN	MON	TUE	WED	THU	FRI	SAT
1	2	3	4	5	6	7
8	9	10	11	12	13	14
15	16	17	18	19	20	21
22	23	24	25	26	27	28
29	30					

B **PAIR WORK.** Tell your partner about your choice. Where is it? When is it?

C 🎧 **SOUND BITES. Read along silently as you listen to a natural conversation.**

EVAN: Do you want to see a concert Saturday? Guitar Wolf's at Maxwell's.

MIKE: Well, thanks, but that's not for me. I'm not really a rock fan.

EVAN: What about Sergio Mendes? He's playing Saturday at the Downbeat.

MIKE: Now that's more my style!

EVAN: Great! There's a show at eleven thirty.

MIKE: Eleven thirty? That's past my bedtime!

EVAN: No problem. There's an early show at eight.

MIKE: Perfect. See you then.

D **Match the sentences with the same meaning.**

_____ **1.** "That's past my bedtime."   **a.** I don't think I want to go to that.

_____ **2.** "That's not for me."   **b.** I like that better.

_____ **3.** "That's more my style."   **c.** That's too late.

E **Read the Garnet City weekend listings on page 16 again. Check ✔ true, false, or no information.**

	true	false	no information
1. Pilar Montenegro is playing at the Downbeat.	☐	☐	☐
2. Sergio Mendes tickets cost $25.	☐	☐	☐
3. Symphony Hall is on First Avenue.	☐	☐	☐
4. Guitar Wolf plays classical music.	☐	☐	☐

WHAT ABOUT YOU?

Are you a music fan? What kind of music do you like? Check the boxes.

☐ Latin   ☐ Rock   ☐ Other _____

☐ Classical   ☐ Jazz

PAIR WORK. Compare your choices. Do you like the same kind of music?

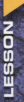

1 ▶ Accept or Decline an Invitation

🎧 **CONVERSATION**
   MODEL **Read and listen.**

A: Are you free on Friday? *Married on Main Street* is at the Film Forum.

B: Really? I'd love to go. What time?

A: At seven ten.

To decline . . .

B: Really? I'd love to go, but I'm busy on Friday.

A: Too bad. Maybe some other time.

🎧 **Rhythm and intonation practice**

Ⓐ **GRAMMAR.** **Prepositions of time and place**

When's the concert? What time's the movie?

Prepositions of time

on	in	at
on Saturday	in May	at 8:30
on June 7th	in 2003	at noon
on Saturday, June 5th	in the summer	at midnight
on Friday morning	in the morning	

Where's the play?

Prepositions of place

on	in	at
on Fifth Avenue	in Mexico	at the Film Forum
on the corner	in Osaka	at work
on the street	in the park	at school
	in the neighborhood	at the theater

Contractions
When's = When is
What time's = What time is
Where's = Where is

0291172

GRAMMAR BOOSTER
PAGE G3
For more . . .

Ⓑ **Complete the e-mail message with prepositions of time and place.**

From:	val670@telcalm.net
To:	hiroko_une@global.jp
Subject:	African music concert

Hi Hiroko: Are you busy _____ Monday night? There's a free concert of African music right near your office _____ the Stern Art Center. Sounds like a great show! It starts _____ 7:30. I'll be _____ work until 5:00, but I could meet you _____ 5:15 or 5:30 _____ the corner of Grand and Crane. We could have something to eat before the concert. What do you think? The price is right! —Val

C ⌒ VOCABULARY. Entertainment events. Listen and practice.

| a movie | a play | a concert | a talk | an art exhibit |

THE FILM FORUM PRESENTS
MARRIED ON MAIN STREET
Friday night only! 7:10

HAMLET
THURSDAY
AND
FRIDAY
7:30 PM
REED
THEATER

BLUES EXPLOSION
THIS SATURDAY AT 12:00
ELLIOT PARK

BOOK WORLD

BRAD McFEE
AUTHOR OF
"TRAVELING
ALONE"
THURSDAY
AT
5:30

BEEKMAN GALLERY
"ART OF THE SIXTIES"
OPENING RECEPTION
TUESDAY 8:00 PM

D ▷ PAIR WORK. Ask and answer questions about the events in the pictures above. Use <u>When</u>, <u>What time</u>, and <u>Where</u>.

❝ Where's the movie? ❞

❝ It's at the Film Forum. ❞

E ⌒ LISTENING COMPREHENSION. Listen to the conversations about entertainment events. Then listen again and complete the chart.

	Kind of event	Time of event
1.	a talk	11:30
2.		
3.		
4.		

CONVERSATION PAIR WORK

Invite your partner to an event. Use these events or other events in <u>your</u> town.

A: Are you free _____? _____ is at _____.

B: _____ ...

Continue the conversation in your <u>own</u> way.

Melbourne
WEEKEND ENTERTAINMENT

MOVIES — *Like Water for Chocolate,* Cine Metro, Sat. / Sun. 8:55

MUSIC — **The Noyz Boyz,** The Garage, Fri. Midnight

TALKS — **Novelist Toni Morrison:** "Love," Book City, Mon. 8:00

THEATER — *My Fair Lady,* Cameo Theater, Every night 8:00

CONTROLLED PRACTICE

Ask for and Give Directions

🎧 CONVERSATION MODEL Read and listen.

A: Excuse me. I'm looking for The Bell Theater.

B: The Bell Theater? Do you know the address?

A: Yes. It's 101 Harper Street.

B: Oh. That's right around the corner, on the left side of the street.

A: Thanks.

If you don't know . . .

B: The Bell Theater? I'm sorry, I'm not from around here.

A: Thanks, anyway.

🎧 **Rhythm and intonation practice**

A 🎧 **VOCABULARY.** **Locations and directions.** **Listen and practice.**

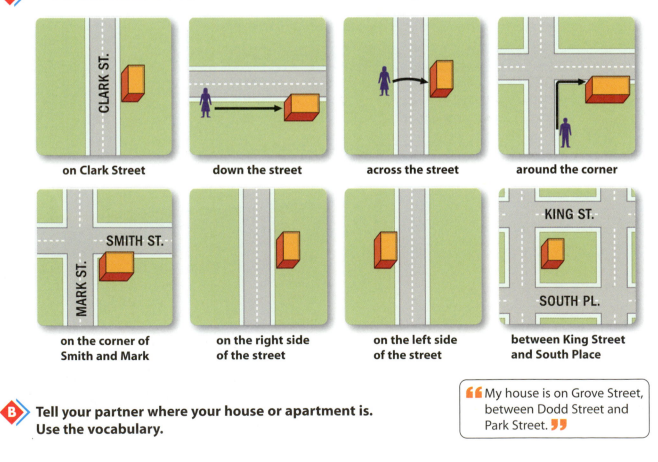

on Clark Street

down the street

across the street

around the corner

on the corner of Smith and Mark

on the right side of the street

on the left side of the street

between King Street and South Place

B Tell your partner where your house or apartment is. Use the vocabulary.

> ❝My house is on Grove Street, between Dodd Street and Park Street. ❞

C ▷ **PAIR WORK.** Practice asking about these locations and giving directions.

- The Bell Theater
- The Film Forum
- Book World
- The Dance Palace
- Taft Symphony Hall
- Moonbucks Coffee 1
- Moonbucks Coffee 2
- The Piermont Museum of Art

Where's Book World?

It's on the corner of Holly Boulevard and Second Avenue.

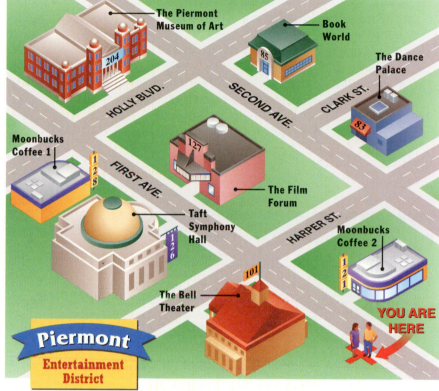

D ▷ 🎧 **PRONUNCIATION.** Rising intonation to confirm information.
Repeat information with rising intonation to be sure you understand.
Listen. Then listen again and repeat.

The public library? ↗   200 Main Street? ↗   The mall? ↗

CONVERSATION PAIR WORK

Ask for and give directions. Use the Piermont map or a map of <u>your</u> town or neighborhood. Start like this:

A: Excuse me. I'm looking for _____.

B: _____? _____ …

Continue the conversation in your <u>own</u> way.

3 ◢ Make Plans to See an Event

A 🎧 **LISTENING COMPREHENSION.** Listen to the phone calls about events at an international arts festival. Then write either <u>a concert</u>, <u>a talk</u>, or <u>a play</u>.

1. _____   2. _____   3. _____

B 🎧 Now look at the March 9th event listings on the festival website. Listen to the phone calls again. Complete the event times and ticket prices.

Barrington International Arts Festival

Barrington International Arts Festival

login   update me

Saturday, March 9

Indian Ocean
INDIA

A blend of Indian classical, rock, jazz, and reggae. When traditional Indian music meets rock guitars, the result is Indian Ocean—the unique sound of India today.

when _8:30 pm_
where Barrington Festival Main Stage
price US $ _____

Copenhagen
NEW ZEALAND

Harborview Theater presents Michael Frayn's Tony Award–winning play. *Copenhagen* explores the impact of scientific progress on modern life.

"This tremendous new play is a piece of history, an intellectual thriller, and a psychological investigation." —*Sunday Times*, UK

when _____ pm and _____ pm
where Harborview Theater
price US $ _____

John Banville
IRELAND

Irish author John Banville talks about his new novel, *The Untouchable*, about British spy Anthony Blunt. "Brilliant"… "exquisitely written." —*Scotland on Sunday*, UK

when _____
where Ambassador Theater
price US $ _____

BARRINGTON FESTIVAL
MAP KEY
1. Main Stage
2. Harborview Theater
3. Ambassador Theater
4. Prescott Park Pavilion
ℹ Festival Information
P Parking

RPX0507 GA GO21014 C .00 ERPX0507

RPX0507 GA   *** Indian Ocean ***

MAR 9 SAT MAR 9 8:30 PM   PCOMP
                              1014

quickticket

INTERACTION · *Let's Go!*

STEP 1. Look at some event listings for March 10.

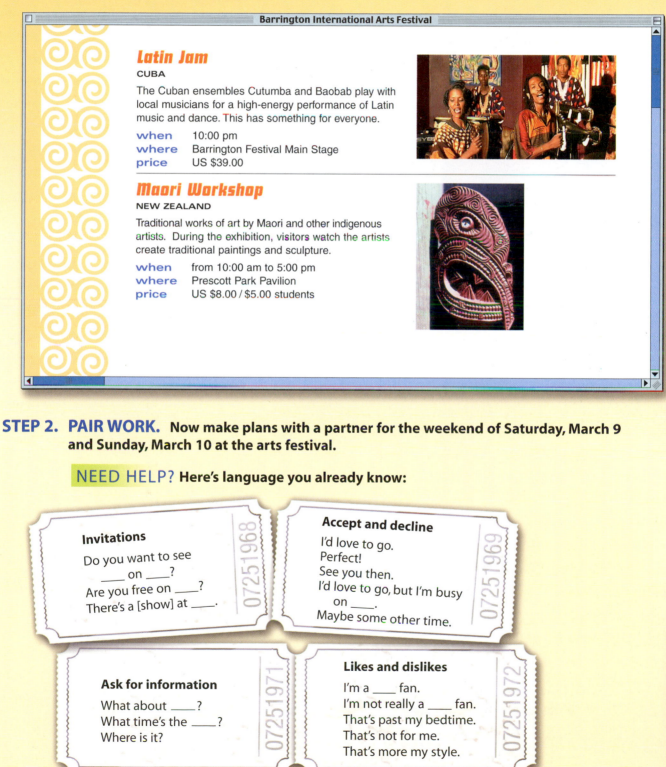

Barrington International Arts Festival

Latin Jam
CUBA

The Cuban ensembles Cutumba and Baobab play with local musicians for a high-energy performance of Latin music and dance. This has something for everyone.

when   10:00 pm
where   Barrington Festival Main Stage
price   US $39.00

Maori Workshop
NEW ZEALAND

Traditional works of art by Maori and other indigenous artists. During the exhibition, visitors watch the artists create traditional paintings and sculpture.

when   from 10:00 am to 5:00 pm
where   Prescott Park Pavilion
price   US $8.00 / $5.00 students

STEP 2. PAIR WORK. Now make plans with a partner for the weekend of Saturday, March 9 and Sunday, March 10 at the arts festival.

NEED HELP? **Here's language you already know:**

Invitations

Do you want to see _____ on _____?
Are you free on _____?
There's a [show] at _____.

07251968

Accept and decline

I'd love to go.
Perfect!
See you then.
I'd love to go, but I'm busy on _____.
Maybe some other time.

07251969

Ask for information

What about _____?
What time's the _____?
Where is it?

07251971

Likes and dislikes

I'm a _____ fan.
I'm not really a _____ fan.
That's past my bedtime.
That's not for me.
That's more my style.

07251972

4 Talk about Musical Tastes

A ► **READING WARM-UP.** **Is music important in your life?**

B ► 🎧 **READING.** *Top Notch* interviewed people about music.
Read what they said.

Music Makes the World Go `Round!

ALFREDO LOPEZ
Mexico, sales manager

► I'm really into music. I listen to it all the time, especially when I travel. Mexico City is my hometown, but I live and work in Veracruz. My favorite music is pop. I prefer CDs to cassettes because the sound quality is good—better than cassettes. But most of all, I like live concerts.

KYUNG-AH SON
Korea, mother and student of English

► I'm a 32-year-old housewife and mother from Seoul. My daughters Han-na and Su-ji keep me very busy all day long, so I don't have much time to listen to music. I listen when they go to sleep. I like dance music, but I don't have much time to dance!

SANDRA PIKE
Canada, managing editor

► I'm from St. Johns, Newfoundland, but I live in New York right now. I'm a big rock fan. I also love choral music and R&B, but I always come back to rock. At work, I listen to music, quietly, if the work isn't too complicated. I recently went to a Rolling Stones concert in New York. It was fantastic!

SOURCE: authentic *Top Notch* interviews

C ► Read about the people again. Check ☑ each statement <u>true</u>, <u>false</u>, or <u>no information</u>. Then explain your answers.

	true	false	no information
1. Mr. Lopez likes cassettes better than CDs.	☐	☐	☐
2. Mrs. Son listens to music all day long.	☐	☐	☐
3. Ms. Pike doesn't like classical music.	☐	☐	☐

D ► **WHAT ABOUT YOU?** Who are you like—Mr. Lopez, Mrs. Son, or Ms. Pike?

> 66 I'm like Alfredo Lopez. I'm really into music. 99

STEP 1. Take the music survey.

TOP NOTCH MUSIC SURVEY

Are you a music fan?
○ yes   ○ no

What's your favorite kind of music?
○ rock   ○ pop   ○ jazz
○ R&B   ○ Latin   ○ classical
○ rap / hip-hop   ○ other _____

When do you listen to music?
○ all the time   ○ when I study
○ when I drive   ○ when I work
   ○ other _____

Do you go to concerts?
○ yes   ○ no

How do you listen to music?
○ cassettes   ○ CDs   ○ Internet
○ radio   ○ other

How many CDs or cassettes do you own?
○ none   ○ 1–50   ○ 50–100
○ 100–200   ○ more than 200

Your age [optional]
○ under 20   ○ 20–30
○ 31–40   ○ over 40

STEP 2. PAIR WORK. Compare surveys with your partner. Summarize your answers and your partner's answers on the notepad.

About me	About my partner
I'm a hip-hop fan.	Her favorite music is hip-hop.

STEP 3. DISCUSSION. Use your notepad to tell the class about yourself and your partner.

My partner and I are both hip-hop fans.

FREE PRACTICE

UNIT 2
CHECKPOINT

 A **LISTENING COMPREHENSION.** Listen to the conversations about events. Complete the chart.

Kind of event	Time of event
1.	
2.	
3.	

B Complete each sentence with the name of the event.

1. This _____ is the most popular of the season.

2. Whose paintings are at the _____?

3. Tonight's _____ is the Mexico City String Quartet.

4. Dr. Benson is giving a _____ on the native plants of the desert. Do you want to go?

5. I'm watching my favorite _____. It just came out on DVD!

C Complete the answers.

1. **2.** **3.** **4.**

1. Where's the bookstore? It's _____.
2. Where's the art exhibit? It's _____.
3. Where's the movie theater? It's _____.
4. Where's the house? It's _____.

D **WRITING.** Write about yourself and **your** tastes in music.

> My name is Kazu Sato. I'm from Nagoya.
> I'm a classical music fan. I love Mozart.

 TOP NOTCH SONG
"Going Out"
Lyrics on last book page.

TOP NOTCH PROJECT
Bring in the entertainment page of your local newspaper. Choose an event. Then write a short note or e-mail message to a classmate inviting him or her to the event. Describe the location of the event.

TOP NOTCH WEBSITE
For Unit 2 online activities, visit the *Top Notch* Companion Website at www.longman.com/topnotch.

UNIT WRAP-UP

- **Vocabulary.** Look at the ads. Then close your book and write the events you remember.

- **Grammar.** Ask and answer questions with <u>Where</u>, <u>When</u>, and <u>What time</u>.

- **Social language.** Make plans, suggestions, and invitations. Discuss your likes and dislikes.

OCTOBER 14   **Bedford News**   page 39

TODAY'S ENTERTAINMENT

"MAKES YOU LAUGH UNTIL YOU CRY"
—Alice Cabezon, *PERSON MAGAZINE*

DAVID CILLY IN

Past My Bedtime

BEDFORD MOVIE THEATER 1   7:00, 9:05, 11:10   **555-CINE**

LETHAL NOISE

NEWSTIME
"POWERFUL"

"May be one of the few horror movies that actually horrify"
—Vincent Frutilla

PLAZA THEATER
238-FLIX
9:30, midnight

OTHER LISTINGS

TALKS

Tina Truffle, *Food for Thought,* lecture, discussion, book signing. The Bookworm Bookstore, second floor cafe, 6:45 pm.

MUSIC

Saint Louis Symphony Orchestra, David Amado, conductor; Amy Oshiro, violin. Beethoven Violin Concerto; Symphony No. 6,"Pastoral." Powel Symphony Hall, 8:00 pm.

Electric Mayhem, rock concert. The Cat Club, Midnight.

PLAYS

Phantom of the Opera. Metroplex, Hill Street Mall, 8:55 pm.

✔ **Now I can ...**

- ☐ accept or decline an invitation.
- ☐ ask for and give directions.
- ☐ make plans to see an event.
- ☐ talk about musical tastes.

27

Talking about Families

UNIT GOALS

1 Describe your family
2 Ask about family members
3 Compare people
4 Talk about small families and large familie

A ▷ **TOPIC PREVIEW.** Do you have lots of photos?
Look at Linda's photo album.

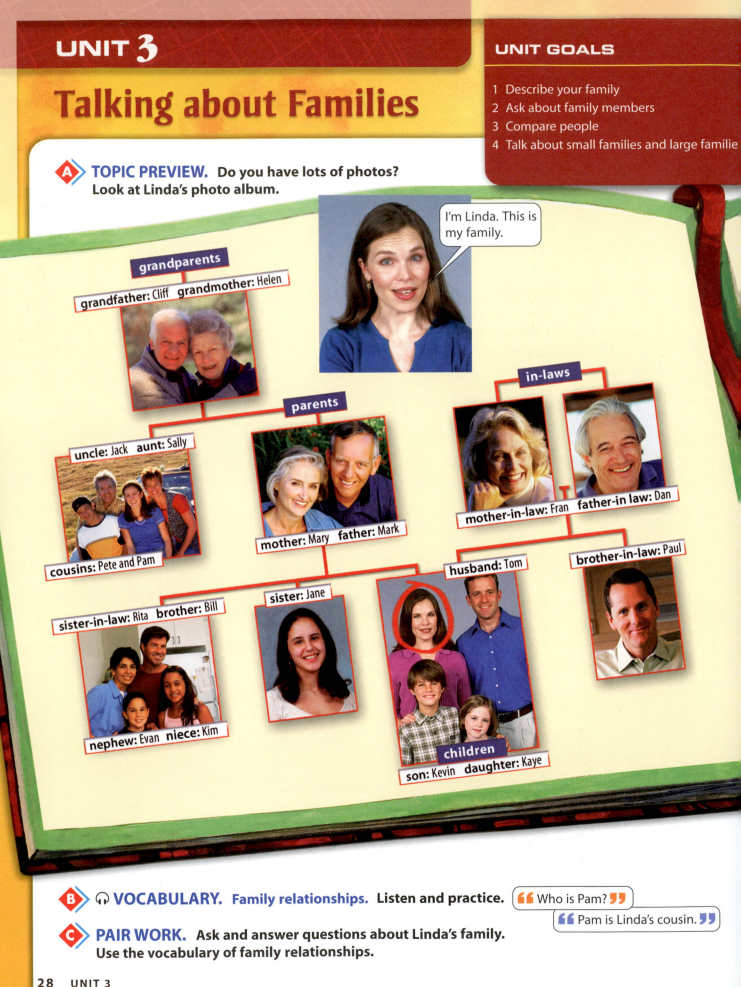

I'm Linda. This is my family.

grandparents
grandfather: Cliff grandmother: Helen

parents

in-laws

uncle: Jack aunt: Sally

mother: Mary father: Mark

mother-in-law: Fran father-in law: Dan

cousins: Pete and Pam

husband: Tom

brother-in-law: Paul

sister-in-law: Rita brother: Bill

sister: Jane

nephew: Evan niece: Kim

children
son: Kevin daughter: Kaye

B ▷ 🎧 **VOCABULARY.** **Family relationships.** **Listen and practice.**

❝ Who is Pam? ❞
❝ Pam is Linda's cousin. ❞

C ▷ **PAIR WORK.** Ask and answer questions about Linda's family.
Use the vocabulary of family relationships.

D 🎧 **SOUND BITES.** Read along silently as you listen to a natural conversation.

ANNA: What are you up to?

MAY: I have some photos of my family. Come take a look.

ANNA: Oh, great! Let me see.

• • •

ANNA: Who's that guy?

MAY: That's my older brother. He works for World Tech in London.

ANNA: Really! And who are those two? They're really cute!

MAY: Oh, those are my sister's kids. That's her right here. They live in Hong Kong.

E Check ☑ **true**, **false**, or **no information**.

	true	false	no information
1. Anna has a large family.	☐	☐	☐
2. May has a husband.	☐	☐	☐
3. May's older brother lives in Hong Kong.	☐	☐	☐
4. May is an aunt.	☐	☐	☐
5. Anna thinks May's sister's kids are cute.	☐	☐	☐

WHAT ABOUT **YOU?**

Complete the chart with names of people in your family.

grandparents	
parents	
in-laws	
sisters and brothers	
nieces and nephews	
husband or wife	
children	
aunts and uncles	
cousins	

Tell the class about your family.

❝ My parents are Blanche and Herbert. I have two brothers, David and Paul. ❞

1 Describe Your Family

A: Tell me something about your family.

B: Sure. What do you want to know?

A: Well, do you have any brothers or sisters?

B: I have two older brothers and a younger sister.

A: Do they look like you?

B: Not really.

🎧 **Rhythm and intonation practice**

A **GRAMMAR.** The simple present tense

Affirmative statements

I **live** in Rio.
We **have** two children
They **work** in a school.

He **lives** in Tokyo.
She **has** four sisters.
Sam **works** in an office.

Negative statements

I **don't live** in Japan.

She **doesn't live** in Mexico.

<u>Yes</u> / <u>no</u> questions

Do you **have** any nieces and nephews?
Does he **live** near her parents?

Short answers

Yes, I do. / No, I don't.
Yes, he does. / No, he doesn't.

GRAMMAR BOOSTER
PAGE G4
For more . . .

B Complete the questions and answers with the simple present tense.

1. (have) **A:** _____ your cousin _____ any children?

   B: Yes, she _____. She _____ a son and a daughter.

2. (live) **A:** _____ your grandparents _____ in Vancouver?

   B: No, they _____. They _____ in Seattle.

3. (work) **A:** _____ your father _____ in Caracas?

   B: Yes, he _____. He _____ at a bank.

4. (look) **A:** _____ your sisters _____ like you?

   B: No, they _____. They _____ like our father.

5. (like) **A:** _____ your brother _____ rock music?

   B: Yes, he _____. He _____ rock music very much.

🎧 **VOCABULARY.** **Marital status and relationships.** **Listen and practice.**

They're **single**.

They're **married**.

They're **divorced**.

She's **widowed**.

He's **an only child**.

They're **twins**.

D 🎧 **LISTENING COMPREHENSION.** **Listen to the conversations carefully.**
Use the vocabulary to complete the statements about the people.

1. He's ___married___.
2. They're _____.
3. She's _____.

4. She's _____.
5. They're _____.
6. He's _____.

CONVERSATION PAIR WORK

Describe your family. Use the guide, or create a new conversation.

A: Tell me something about your family.
B: _____. What do you want to know?
A: Well, do you have any _____?
B: _____ …

Continue the conversation in your <u>own</u> way.

To continue:
How about children?
Aunts and uncles?
Nieces and nephews?

2

Ask about Family Members

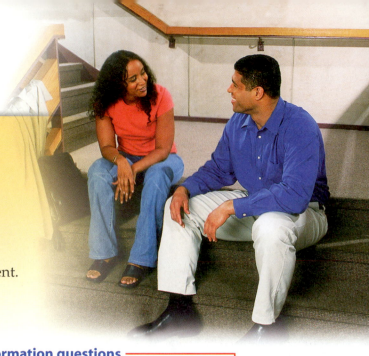

🎧 CONVERSATION MODEL Read and listen.

A: So what does your sister do?

B: She's a graphic designer. She works at Panorama Designs.

A: That's great! How about your brother?

B: He doesn't have a job right now. He's a student.

🎧 **Rhythm and intonation practice**

A **GRAMMAR.** The simple present tense: information questions

What does your younger brother **do**?	He works in a bank.
What do your parents **do**?	They're artists.
Where do your grandparents **live**?	They live near me.
Where does your sister **live**?	She lives in Toronto.
When do you **see** your cousins?	We visit them every summer.
How many children **do** you **have**?	I have two—a boy and a girl.
Who works at Panorama?	My sister does.

GRAMMAR BOOSTER

PAGE G5
For more . . .

B **Complete the conversations with the simple present tense.**

1. **A:** My father _____ in a restaurant.

   B: Really? _____ he do?

   A: He's a chef.

2. **A:** My brother _____ with his family in Sydney.

   B: _____ kids _____ he have?

   A: Three. I've got three nephews.

   B: That's great!

Sydney, Australia

3. **A:** _____ your sister live?

   B: She _____ in Bangkok with her family.

   A: _____ see them?

   B: I visit them every year.

Bangkok, Thailand

4. **A:** _____ your in-laws do?

   B: They both _____ at City Hospital. They're doctors.

   A: Really? Is your wife a doctor, too?

   B: No, she _____ in an office.

5. **A:** My older sister and my younger brother both _____ kids.

   B: _____ nieces and nephews _____ you _____?

   A: I have six. Four nieces and two nephews.

6. **A:** Where _____ your husband _____?

   B: He works at Harry's Shoes, on Franklin Street.

   A: Oh, I know that place! What _____ he _____ there?

   B: He's a manager.

C **PAIR WORK.** On a separate sheet of paper, write three <u>yes</u> / <u>no</u> questions and three information questions for your partner. Write answers to your partner's questions.

> Do you have any brothers or sisters?

> Yes, I do. I have three older brothers
> and two younger sisters.

D 🎧 **PRONUNCIATION.** Blending sounds. Listen and repeat the questions.

/dʌʃi/
1. <mark>Does she</mark> have any children? What <mark>does she</mark> do? /dʌʃi/

/dʌzi/
2. <mark>Does he</mark> live near you? What <mark>does he</mark> do? /dʌzi/

CONVERSATION
PAIR WORK

Ask about your partner's family. Use the guide, or create a new conversation.

A: So what does your ____ do?

B: ____.

A: ____. How about your ____?

B: ____ …

Continue the conversation in your <u>own</u> way.

Compare People

A 🎧 **VOCABULARY.** Similarities and differences. Listen and practice.

How are you <u>alike</u>?

We **look alike**.

We wear **similar** clothes.

We **both** like basketball. She likes basketball, and I do **too**.

She doesn't like fish, and I don't **either**.

How are you <u>different</u>?

We **look different**.

We wear **different** clothes.

He likes rock music, **but** I like classical.

He likes coffee, **but** I don't.

B 🎧 **LISTENING COMPREHENSION.** Listen to Frank Pascal talk about himself and his brother, Philippe. Listen for their similarities and differences. Check ✔ the statements that are true.

Frank and Philippe . . .	
1. ☐ live in the same country	☑ live in different countries
2. ☐ look alike	☐ look different
3. ☐ have similar occupations	☐ have very different occupations
4. ☐ like the same music	☐ like different music
5. ☐ read the same things	☐ read different things
6. ☐ like the same kinds of movies	☐ like different kinds of movies

INTERACTION • *It's All in the Family*

STEP 1. On the notepad, write sentences comparing yourself to one member of your family.

The person's name and relationship to you:

How are you alike?   How are you different?

STEP 2. PAIR WORK. First tell your partner about the person you wrote about. Then discuss other people in your families.

> ❝ My brother and I are different ... ❞

NEED HELP? Here's language you already know:

Ask about families

Tell me about your ____.
Do you have any ____?
How many ____ do you have?
How about ____?

How old ____?
What do / does your ____ do?
Where do / does your ____ live?

Similarities and differences

How are you alike?
How are you different?
Do you look alike?
Do you both ____?

STEP 3. WRITING. Write a paragraph comparing two people in your family.

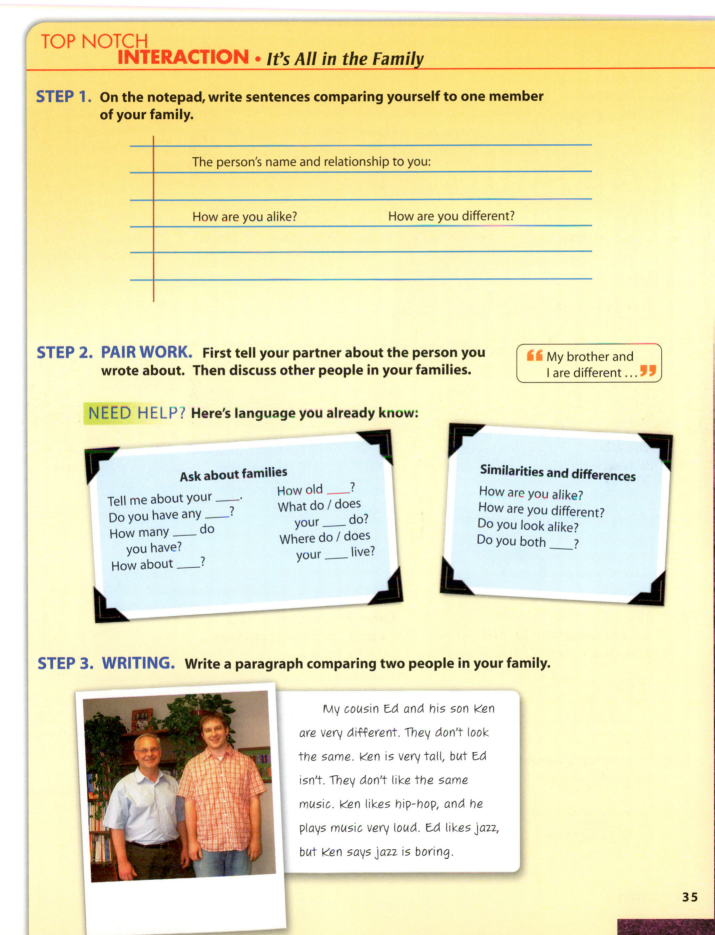

My cousin Ed and his son Ken are very different. They don't look the same. Ken is very tall, but Ed isn't. They don't like the same music. Ken likes hip-hop, and he plays music very loud. Ed likes jazz, but Ken says jazz is boring.

FREE PRACTICE

LESSON

4 *Talk about Small Families and Large Families*

A **READING WARM-UP.** Do you come from a small family or a large family?

B 🎧 **READING.** Read about large and small families.

Families Come in All Sizes

On November 18, 1997, Bobbi and Kenny McCaughey of the United States were the happy parents of one child—their daughter Mikayla. The next day, they had eight children. Bobbi gave birth to septuplets—three more daughters and four new sons. At first it was very hard. They lived in a very small house and they needed lots of help. Now it is better. They live in a big house and the children help with the housework.

Barry and Julia Rollings of Canberra, Australia started with just two daughters: Alix and Briony. Then, between 1991 and 1998, they adopted six more children—five sons and one daughter. Barry also has four adult children from his first marriage. People always ask them, "How many kids do you have now?"

Julia says, "I love my family and my life!" And she adds, "Barry likes housework."

In traditional Chinese culture, families were very large. But in mainland China today, with a population of over 1,000,000,000 people, the government has a one-child policy: in most places, a family can have only one child. In the future, there will be no aunts, uncles, or cousins. Why? Because there will be no sisters or brothers.

Many people don't agree with the one-child policy. But all agree that one advantage of a small family is that parents have more money for their children.

SOURCE: www.geocities.com/juro/madhouse and www.msnbc.com

C Now read the following statements. Figure out if they are true or false, based on the information in the reading.

	true	false	no information given
1. Septuplets are seven children born at the same time.	☐	☐	☐
2. Alix and Briony Rollings are twins.	☐	☐	☐
3. Julia Rollings is Barry's first wife.	☐	☐	☐
4. The traditional Chinese family was a one-child family.	☐	☐	☐

D According to the reading, what are the advantages and disadvantages of small and large families? Match the information in the two columns.

_____ **1.** an advantage of a small family

_____ **2.** an advantage of a large family

_____ **3.** a disadvantage of a small family

_____ **4.** a disadvantage of a large family

a. Families have more money.

b. There are too many people in the house.

c. Children don't have brothers, sisters, aunts, uncles, or cousins.

d. Children help their parents with the housework.

TOP NOTCH
INTERACTION • *Small or Large?*

STEP 1. Write some more advantages and disadvantages of small and large families on the notepad.

A Small Family

Advantages	Disadvantages

A Large Family

Advantages	Disadvantages

STEP 2. DISCUSSION. What kind of family do you prefer: a small family or a large family? Tell your class why.

I prefer a small family because the parents have more time for the children.

I disagree. I think a large family is better. A family with lots of children is a happy family.

A 🎧 **LISTENING COMPREHENSION.** Listen carefully to the people talking about their families. Check ☑ if the person has a big or small family.

	big family	small family
1. Hassan	☐	☐
2. Karen	☐	☐
3. Andrew	☐	☐
4. Sandra	☐	☐

B 🎧 Listen again. How many children are there in each family?

1. _____   2. _____   3. _____   4. _____

C Complete the sentences with the correct word or words.

1. Jason doesn't have any brothers and sisters. He's an _____.

2. Harry is Henry's brother. They have the same birthdate. They are _____.

3. Nick's sister has three daughters. They are Nick's _____.

4. Gary is Teresa's husband. Gary's parents are Teresa's _____.

5. Randy's mother has a niece and a nephew. They are Randy's _____.

6. John and Carl are brothers. John's wife is Carl's _____.

7. Oliva is Ellen's mother. Alice is Ellen's daughter. Oliva is Alice's _____.

D **WRITING.** Read about Susan and Peter Wolf. Then write about them. How are they different? How are they similar?

> Susan Wolf, 28, is the manager of a clothing store in Chicago. She is short and blonde and she wears glasses. Susan is a big fan of classical music. She goes to classical concerts and has lots of classical music CDs. She likes some other kinds of music, too, but she doesn't like hip-hop or rock.
>
> Peter Wolf, 24, is Susan's younger brother. He is a rock musician and lives in Seattle. Peter has blond hair. He is tall and he wears glasses. Peter loves rock music. He doesn't like any other kind of music. He goes to rock concerts and has lots of CDs of rock musicians.

Peter is a rock music fan, but Susan likes classical music.
They both have blond hair.

TOP NOTCH PROJECT
Make a family scrapbook. Bring in photos from home. Tell your class about your family.

TOP NOTCH WEBSITE
For Unit 3 online activities, visit the *Top Notch* Companion Website at www.longman.com/topnotch.

- **Vocabulary.** Look at the Douglas family tree. Talk about the family relationships.
  Kirk Douglas is Michael Douglas's father . . .
- **Grammar.** Ask and answer questions.
  Does Michael Douglas have any brothers or sisters?
- **Writing.** Write about the Douglas family.

The Douglas Family

Anne Douglas

Kirk Douglas
actor

· · · divorced · · ·

Diana Dill
actress

father
David Jones

mother
Pat Jones

half brother
Peter

half brother
Eric

brother
Joel

brother
David

brother
Lyndon

Diandra Douglas
producer

· · · divorced · · ·

Michael Douglas
actor
birthday: Sept. 25

Catherine Zeta-Jones
actress
birthday: Sept. 25

Cameron
actor

Dylan Michael

Carys

SOURCE: www.michaeldouglas.com

✓ **Now I can . . .**
- ☐ describe my family.
- ☐ ask about family members.
- ☐ compare people.
- ☐ talk about small families and large families.

Coping with Technology

UNIT GOALS

1 Suggest a brand or model
2 Express frustration about a machine
3 Describe features of machines
4 Complain when things don't work

A ▷ **TOPIC PREVIEW.** Look at the ad from a shopping catalog. Do you like catalogs that sell electronic gadgets?

THE COMMUNICATOR

สวัสดี
HELLO

RM2000

THE COMMUNICATOR
Pocket electronic talking translator

• Translates from English to eight other world languages.
• Displays text on screen AND correctly pronounces words and phrases.
• Makes world travel a breeze!

COM445 . . . .
see page 46

B ▷ **DISCUSSION.** Is The Communicator a good product? Would you like to have one? Why or why not?

❝ It's great for me. I like to travel. ❞

❝ It's not a good way to learn English. ❞

SOUND BITES. Read along silently as you listen to a natural conversation.

CLAIRE: This printer's driving me crazy!
MARIE: What do you mean?
CLAIRE: It's not working again. It won't print.
MARIE: What's wrong with it?
CLAIRE: I don't know. It's just a lemon!

D Read the conversation carefully. Then check ☑ each statement <u>true</u>, <u>false</u>, or <u>no information</u>.

	true	false	no information
1. The printer is not printing.	☐	☐	☐
2. It's a new printer.	☐	☐	☐
3. Marie doesn't have a printer.	☐	☐	☐
4. A lemon is a good machine.	☐	☐	☐

WHAT ABOUT **YOU?**

What machines drive <u>you</u> crazy? Make a list. Use a dictionary if necessary.

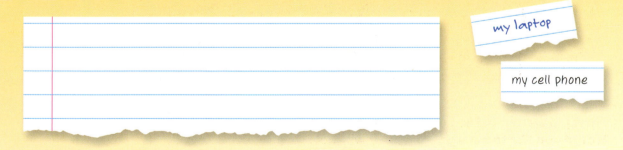

my laptop

my cell phone

PAIR WORK. Compare your lists. Are they the same or different?

1 ▸ Suggest a Brand or Model

LESSON

🎧 CONVERSATION MODEL Read and listen.

A: Hey, Bob! What are <u>you</u> doing here?

B: Hi, Louis. I'm looking for a laptop. Any suggestions?

A: What about a Pell? The X340 is great.

B: Really?

A: Yes. And it's inexpensive.

🎧 Rhythm and intonation practice

🎧 Positive adjectives

pretty good ☺
great ☺☺
terrific ☺☺☺
awesome ☺☺☺☺

Ⓐ GRAMMAR. The present continuous

Use the present continuous for actions in progress now and for some future actions.
Form the present continuous with <u>be</u> and a present participle (base form + <u>-ing</u>).

I**'m looking** for a laptop. (action in progress now)

Tomorrow I**'m going** to Technoland. (future action)

Questions	Answers
Are you looking for a cell phone?	Yes, I am. / No, I'm not.
Is he using the computer?	Yes, he is. / No, he's not.
Are they buying the X340?	Yes, they are. / No, they're not.
What are you doing?	We're getting a new printer.
Who's buying a new cell phone?	My brother is.

GRAMMAR BOOSTER

PAGES G5–G7
For more . . .

Ⓑ Read the sentences and questions. Check ☑ Action in progress or Future action.

	Action in progress	Future action
1. What are you doing this weekend?		✔
2. I'm busy right now. I'm answering my e-mails.		
3. He's leaving in thirty minutes. Hurry!		
4. Beth is at the library. She's studying for an exam.		
5. Josh isn't home right now. He's shopping for a laptop.		

C 🎧 **VOCABULARY.** **Electronics.** Listen and practice. Which machines do you have? Which machines are you looking for?

a TV

a laptop

a PDA

a printer

a cell phone

a CD burner

D Complete each conversation with the present continuous.

1. **A:** _____ to Technoland this afternoon?
   <u>Marian / go</u>

   B: Yes, _____ a new CD burner.
   <u>she / buy</u>

2. **A:** What time _____ tomorrow?
   <u>you / leave</u>

   B: _____ the 5:30 train.
   <u>I / take</u>

3. **A:** _____ for a new laptop?
   <u>Jim / look</u>

   B: No, _____ for a PDA.
   <u>he / shop</u>

4. **A:** _____ anything right now?
   <u>you / do</u>

   B: Yes, _____ the house.
   <u>I / clean</u>

E 🎧 **PRONUNCIATION.** Intonation of <u>yes</u> / <u>no</u> and information questions. Listen and check ☑ the boxes for rising or falling intonation.

☐ ☐ **1.** What time are you leaving?

☐ ☐ **2.** Are you going today?

☐ ☐ **3.** When is she returning?

☐ ☐ **4.** Is Julie buying a laptop?

CONVERSATION
PAIR WORK

Suggest a brand or a model. Use the pictures and the guide, or create a new conversation.

A: Hey, ____! What are *you* doing here?
B: Hi, I'm looking for ____. Any suggestions?
A: What about ____? The ____ is ____.
B: Really?
A: Yes. And it's ____.

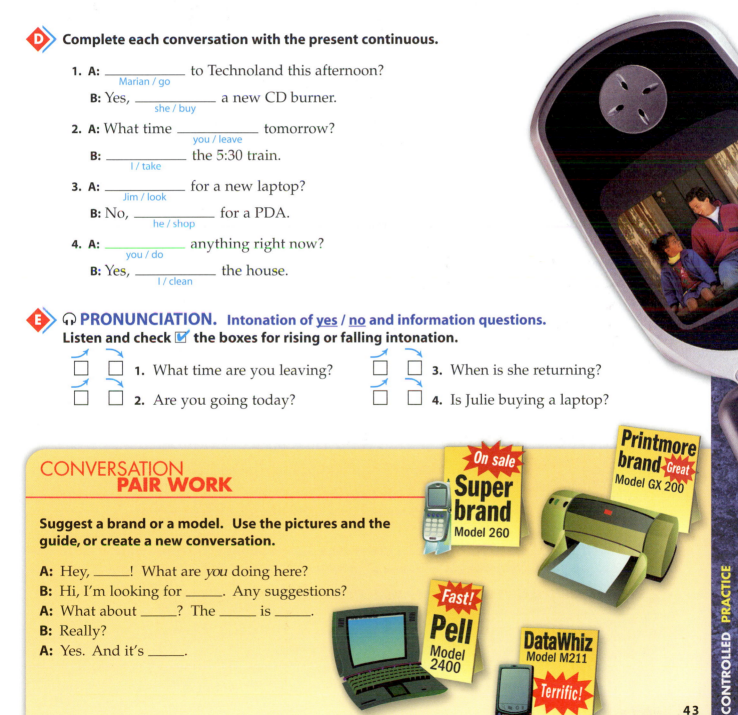

On sale
Super brand Model 260

Printmore brand Great Model GX 200

Fast!
Pell Model 2400

DataWhiz Model M211
Terrific!

Express Frustration about a Machine

MODEL Read and listen.

A: Hello?
B: Hi, Ed. How's it going?
A: Fine, thanks. But my CD player's not working. It's driving me crazy!
B: I'm sorry to hear that. What brand is it?
A: A Tunebox. It's awful.

🎧 **Rhythm and intonation practice**

🎧 **Ways to sympathize**
I'm sorry to hear that.
That's too bad.
That's a shame.

🎧 **Negative descriptions**
pretty bad
terrible
a piece of junk
awful
a lemon

A 🎧 **VOCABULARY. Machines at home and at work. Listen and practice.**

a microwave oven   a coffee maker   a hair dryer   a CD player   a fax machine   a photocopier

B Complete each statement with the name of a machine from the vocabulary.

1. You use a _____ to make copies of documents and pictures.
2. I just got a new battery-operated _____ so I can listen to music outside.
3. I love my new _____. It can cook a chicken in minutes!
4. You use a _____ to send a copy of your document to someone else over the telephone line.
5. This _____ is making a funny sound. Maybe I'll just go out with wet hair.

C 🎧 **LISTENING COMPREHENSION. Listen to the conversations. Write the name of each machine. Do _you_ have problems with one of these machines too? Tell your partner.**

	Machine
1.	CD player
2.	
3.	

	Machine
4.	
5.	
6.	

D ▷ **VOCABULARY BUILDING.** Make a list of the machines and appliances in the pictures. Add machines and appliances you have in <u>your</u> house. Use a bilingual dictionary for words you don't know in English.

in the kitchen

_____
_____
_____

in the living room

_____
_____
_____

in the bedroom

_____
_____
_____

in the bathroom

_____
_____
_____

CONVERSATION PAIR WORK

Express frustration about a machine. Use your own brands. Use the guide, or create a new conversation.

A: Hello?

B: Hi, _____. How's it going?

A: Fine, thanks. But my _____ not working. It's driving me crazy!

B: _____. What brand is it?

A: _____. It's _____.

45   **CONTROLLED PRACTICE**

Describe Features of Machines

A ▶ **READING WARM-UP.** Do you like electronic gadgets? Where do you buy them?

B ▶ 🎧 **READING.** Read and listen to the ad. Then close your book and write two sentences about the Communicator.

THE COMMUNICATOR

The pocket electronic talking translator!!

Translates to AND from English and eight other world languages. Displays text on screen and correctly pronounces words for you.

FEATURES

- It's **convenient**. Makes reading and speaking a foreign language easy and fast. Just press a button and get a translation. Save time!
- It's **popular**. Used by more travelers than any other pocket translator.
- It's **portable**. Lighter and smaller than a dictionary. Just put the Communicator in your pocket or purse and carry it anywhere.
- It's **guaranteed**. Use The Communicator for one full year. If you are not happy with our product, just return it and we will refund your money!

Battery operated. Uses 2 AAA batteries (included). Weighs just 5.5 oz. (.15 kg.)

46

C ▶ 🎧 **LISTENING COMPREHENSION.** Listen to the radio ads. Then listen again. Check the adjectives.

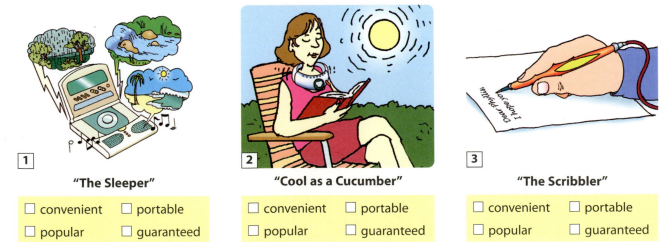

1
"The Sleeper"

☐ convenient ☐ portable
☐ popular ☐ guaranteed

2
"Cool as a Cucumber"

☐ convenient ☐ portable
☐ popular ☐ guaranteed

3
"The Scribbler"

☐ convenient ☐ portable
☐ popular ☐ guaranteed

D ▶ **PAIR WORK.** Which product would <u>you</u> like to have? Why?

Complete each sentence with an adjective from the reading and listening.

1. If this hair dryer stops working, you can get your money back. It's _____.

2. This TV is _____; it's so small and light you can carry it anywhere!

3. This new cell phone is very _____. Everybody wants one.

4. I use the Coffee Pro 200 to make coffee at home. It's easy and it saves time. It's _____.

TOP NOTCH
INTERACTION • *It's the Latest Thing!*

STEP 1. DISCUSSION. Read and discuss the ads. Do you like these products? Why? Why not?

DRIVER ALARM

Avoid accidents. Alarm rings if you start to fall asleep while you are driving. Battery powered. Guaranteed to keep you awake.

SPOTLIGHT PEN

When it's too dark to see what you're writing, it's not too dark for the Spotlight Pen. The amazing Spotlight Pen lights up your paper. Won't disturb those who are sleeping nearby. Guaranteed.

STEP 2. Write your own machines, gadgets, and appliances on the notepad.

Item	Brand	Description
electric teapot	Quick-T	It's fast and convenient.
1.		
2.		
3.		

STEP 3. GROUP WORK. Tell your classmates about your machines. Write your lists on the board. Discuss the products.

NEED HELP? Here's language you already know:

pretty bad   awful
terrible   a lemon
a piece of junk
☹

great   terrific
awesome   fast
popular   convenient
guaranteed   pretty good
☺

4 Complain When Things Don't Work

LESSON

A 🎧 **VOCABULARY.** Ways to state a complaint. Listen and practice.

The window **won't open / close**.

The iron **won't turn on**.

The air-conditioning **won't turn off**.

The fridge is **making a funny sound**.

The toilet **won't flush**.

The sink **is clogged**.

B 🎧 **LISTENING COMPREHENSION.** Listen to the conversations between hotel guests and the front desk. Then listen again and write the room number for each complaint.

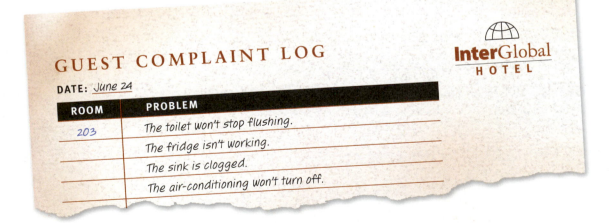

GUEST COMPLAINT LOG

InterGlobal HOTEL

DATE: *June 24*

ROOM	PROBLEM
203	The toilet won't stop flushing.
	The fridge isn't working.
	The sink is clogged.
	The air-conditioning won't turn off.

C **DISCUSSION.** Look at the vocabulary pictures and the problems on the Guest Complaint Log. Which are bad problems? Which are not so bad? Explain.

INTERACTION • *"Front Desk, Can I Help You?"*

STEP 1. **Find all the problems in the hotel. Write them on the notepad.**

Room or place	Problem

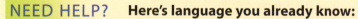

STEP 2. PAIR WORK. Role-play conversations between the hotel guests and the front desk clerk.

❝ Front desk. Can I help you? ❞

❝ This is room 211. Our door won't open. ❞

NEED HELP?   Here's language you already know:

Telephone language

Hello?
This is room ___.
Can I call you back?
Bye.

State a problem

won't open / close
won't turn on / off
won't stop flushing
isn't working
is clogged
is making a funny sound
is driving me crazy

Respond

What's the problem?
I'm sorry to hear that.

A 🎧 **LISTENING COMPREHENSION.** Listen to the conversations about problems with machines. Then listen again. Write the problem.

1. _____
2. _____
3. _____

> The printer is making a funny sound.

B **Write a question in the present continuous.**

☐ **1.** he / talk / on the phone _____?

☐ **2.** Who / use / the computer / right now _____?

☐ **3.** When / Laura / leave _____?

☐ **4.** we / go / to work tomorrow _____?

☐ **5.** When / you / buy / the tickets _____?

☐ **6.** What time / you / leave / for the concert _____?

C Check ✓ the questions in exercise B that have <u>future</u> meaning.

D Write your <u>own</u> answer to each question with real information. Use the present continuous. Use contractions.

1. Where are you going tomorrow? **YOU** _____.

2. Where are you eating dinner tonight? **YOU** _____.

3. What are you doing tomorrow? **YOU** _____.

4. What are you doing right now? **YOU** _____.

E Complete each statement with an adjective.

1. Lots of people are buying it. It's _____.

2. It's small enough to fit in your pocket. It's very _____.

3. It only takes a few seconds to do the job. It's _____.

4. It doesn't cost too much. It's very _____.

5. If it stops working, you can get your money back. It's _____.

F **WRITING.** Write a paragraph about a machine that you own. Use your notes on page 47 for ideas.

TOP NOTCH PROJECT
Write and design ads for the best products. Include pictures or photographs. Use the ads in Unit 4 as a model.

TOP NOTCH WEBSITE
For Unit 4 online activities, visit the *Top Notch* Companion Website at www.longman.com/topnotch.

UNIT WRAP-UP

- **Vocabulary.** Look at the picture. Then close your books. Write all the machines you remember.

- **Grammar.** Ask and answer questions about what the people are doing. Use the present continuous.

- **Writing.** Write about the problems in the picture.

We fix anything

Guaranteed

✔ **Now I can ...**

☐ suggest a brand or model.
☐ express frustration about a machine.
☐ describe features of machines.
☐ complain when things don't work.

Eating in, Eating out

UNIT GOALS

1 Discuss what to eat
2 Make food choices
3 Order and pay for a meal
4 Discuss food and health

A) TOPIC PREVIEW. Read the menu. Which foods do you like? Which foods do you dislike?

World Café

Chef and Owner: Ronald Gebert

"The Best Food in the World!" Max Reed, *Journal News*, April 22

Appetizers

Thai grilled shrimp
Mexican black bean soup

Entrées

Brazilian steak
Fried fish Chinese style
Roast chicken

Salads

Mixed green salad
Tomato salad

Desserts

Ice cream
Apple pie
German chocolate cake

Beverages

Coffee • Tea • Soft drinks • Fruit juice
Bottled water

B) Look at the menu again. Check ☑ the information you can find.

- ☑ 1. food choices
- ☐ 2. beverage choices
- ☐ 3. prices
- ☐ 4. the name of the restaurant owner
- ☐ 5. the names of the waiters and waitresses
- ☐ 6. the name of the chef
- ☐ 7. a restaurant review

C 🎧 **SOUND BITES.** Read along silently as you listen to a natural conversation.

WAITER: Are you ready to order? Or do you need some more time?

CUSTOMER: I'm ready. I think I'll start with the black bean soup. Then I'll have the roast chicken. That comes with salad, doesn't it?

WAITER: Yes, it does. And there's also a choice of vegetables. Tonight we have carrots or grilled tomatoes.

CUSTOMER: The carrots, please.

WAITER: Certainly. Anything to drink?

CUSTOMER: I'll have bottled water, no ice.

D Read the conversation carefully again. Then write <u>true</u> or <u>false</u>.

_____ **1.** The customer orders carrots.

_____ **2.** The customer doesn't order soup.

_____ **3.** The chicken comes with salad.

_____ **4.** The chicken comes with a vegetable.

WHAT ABOUT **YOU?**

Look at the menu from the World Café again. Write the items that <u>you</u> would like to order.

appetizer:	
salad:	
entrée / main course:	
dessert:	
beverage:	

PAIR WORK. Compare your choices. Are they the same or different?

1 Discuss What to Eat

CONVERSATION MODEL Read and listen.

A: What is there to eat?
B: Not much. Cheese, bread, ...eggs.
A: Is that all? I'm in the mood for seafood.
B: Sorry. You're out of luck. Let's go out!
A: Good idea!

Rhythm and intonation practice

A GRAMMAR. Count and non-count nouns / there is and there are

Count and non-count nouns

Count nouns name things you can count. They are singular or plural.

singular count noun	plural count noun
an **egg**	ten **eggs**

Non-count nouns name things you can not count. They are not singular or plural. Don't use <u>a</u>, <u>an</u>, or a number with non-count nouns.

rice   NOT ~~a rice~~   NOT ~~rices~~

count nouns
an appetizer   an onion
an apple   an orange
a cookie   a sandwich
an egg   a vegetable

There is and there are

Use <u>there is</u> with non-count nouns and singular count nouns.
Use <u>there are</u> with plural count nouns.

There's milk and an apple in the fridge.

There are oranges, too. But **there aren't** any vegetables.

Use <u>there is</u> with <u>something</u>, <u>anything</u>, or <u>nothing</u>.

Is there anything to eat? No, **there isn't** anything.

non-count nouns
bread   juice   rice
candy   lettuce salt
cheese   meat   seafood
chocolate milk   soup
coffee   pasta   sugar
fruit

GRAMMAR BOOSTER

PAGES G7–G9
For more . . .

B Complete each sentence or question with a form of <u>there is</u> or <u>there are</u>.

1. _Is there_ anything in the fridge?

2. _____ any cookies?

3. I hope _____ no chocolate in this cake. I'm allergic.

4. _____ anything to eat in this house? I'm hungry.

5. _____ eggs in the fridge. We could make an omelette.

6. I don't think _____ any vegetables on the menu.

7. _____ too much sugar in this coffee.

8. _____ enough lettuce to make a salad?

C ⌒ **VOCABULARY BUILDING.** Categories of food. Add another food you know to each list. Then listen and practice.

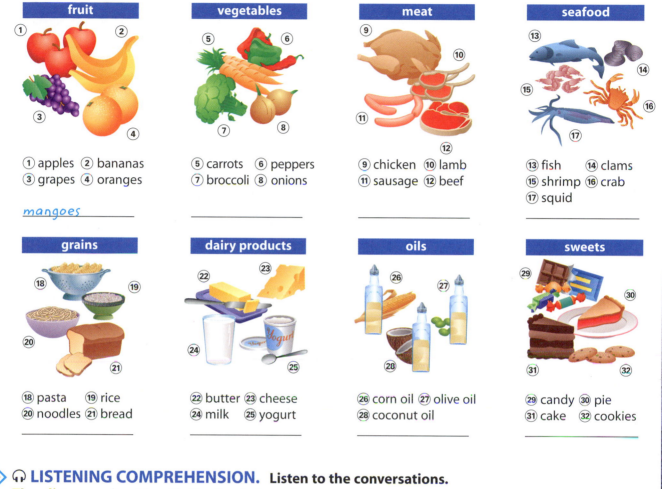

fruit	vegetables	meat	seafood

① apples ② bananas
③ grapes ④ oranges

mangoes

⑤ carrots ⑥ peppers
⑦ broccoli ⑧ onions

⑨ chicken ⑩ lamb
⑪ sausage ⑫ beef

⑬ fish ⑭ clams
⑮ shrimp ⑯ crab
⑰ squid

grains	dairy products	oils	sweets

⑱ pasta ⑲ rice
⑳ noodles ㉑ bread

㉒ butter ㉓ cheese
㉔ milk ㉕ yogurt

㉖ corn oil ㉗ olive oil
㉘ coconut oil

㉙ candy ㉚ pie
㉛ cake ㉜ cookies

D ⌒ **LISTENING COMPREHENSION.** Listen to the conversations. Then listen again. Classify the foods in each conversation.

1. *dairy products*   2. _____   3. _____

4. _____   5. _____   6. _____

CONVERSATION
PAIR WORK

Discuss what to eat. Use foods you like and eat. Use the guide, or create a new conversation.

A: What is there to eat?

B: _____ .

A: Is that all? I'm in the mood for _____ .

B: _____ …

Continue the conversation in your own way.

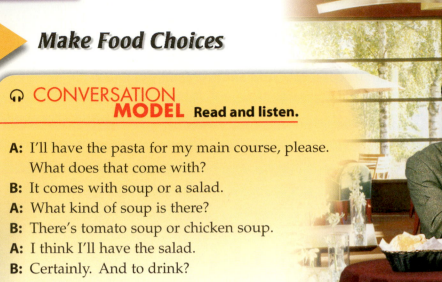

2 LESSON

Make Food Choices

🎧 **CONVERSATION MODEL** Read and listen.

A: I'll have the pasta for my main course, please. What does that come with?
B: It comes with soup or a salad.
A: What kind of soup is there?
B: There's tomato soup or chicken soup.
A: I think I'll have the salad.
B: Certainly. And to drink?
A: Water, please.

🎧 **Rhythm and intonation practice**

A ▷ **GRAMMAR.** A / an / the

a / an
　　It comes with **a salad** and **an appetizer**.

---

the
Use the to name something a second time.
　　A: It comes with a salad.
　　B: OK. I'll have **the salad**.

Also use the to talk about something specific.
　　A: Would you like an appetizer? [not specific]
　　B: Yes. **The fried clams** sound delicious. [specific: they're on the menu]

GRAMMAR BOOSTER

PAGES G9–G10
For more . . .

B ▷ 🎧 **PRONUNCIATION. The.** Compare the pronunciation of **the** before consonant and vowel sounds. Read and listen. Then repeat.

/ə/(before consonant sounds)
the chicken
the soup
the juice
the hot appetizer
the fried eggs

/i/(before vowel sounds)
the orange juice
the onion soup
the apple juice
the appetizer
the eggs

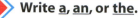 **Write a, an, or the.**

HUSBAND: What do you feel like eating tonight?

WIFE: Well, _____ seafood special sounds delicious. I think I'll order that. What about you?

HUSBAND: I'm not sure. I'm really in the mood for _____ spicy dish.

WIFE: Well, what about _____ Thai chicken? Thai food is usually spicy.

HUSBAND: Sounds good.

HUSBAND: Excuse me! We're ready to order.

WAITER: Certainly. Would you like to start with _____ appetizer or soup? Our soup of the day is tortilla soup—that's _____ Mexican specialty.

HUSBAND: Is _____ tortilla soup spicy?

WAITER: Not very. But we can give you hot pepper sauce to put into it if you'd like.

HUSBAND: OK. I'll have _____ tortilla soup—with the hot sauce on the side.

WIFE: I'll have the same thing, please.

WAITER: And for your main course? We have _____ nice seafood special on _____ menu tonight.

WIFE: Good. I'll have _____ seafood special.

HUSBAND: Hmm. I love Thai food. I'll have _____ Thai chicken.

WAITER: You won't need hot sauce with that, sir!

CONVERSATION
PAIR WORK

Make food choices from the menu with a partner. Use the guide, or create a new conversation.

A: I'll have the _____ for my main course, please. What does that come with?

B: _____.

A: What kind of _____ there?

B: _____.

A: I think I'll have the _____.

B: _____ . And to drink?

A: _____ , please.

Tonight's Specials

Soup   tomato soup
            beef noodle soup

Appetizers
            seafood salad
            grilled vegetables

Main Courses   all come with soup
                   or an appetizer
            grilled chicken
            pasta with clam sauce
            roast lamb

Beverages
            fruit juices   coffee
            bottled water   tea

CONTROLLED PRACTICE

3 Order and Pay for a Meal

A 🎧 **VOCABULARY.** What to say to a waiter or waitress. Listen and practice.

Excuse me!

We're ready to order.

We'll take the check, please.

Is the tip included?   **Do you accept credit cards?**

B 🎧 **LISTENING COMPREHENSION.** Listen to the conversations in a restaurant. Then listen again and predict the next thing the customer will say to the waiter or waitress.

1. ☐ Is the tip included in the check?
2. ☐ Is the tip included?
3. ☐ Excuse me!
4. ☐ Is the tip included?
5. ☐ I'll have the seafood soup, please.

☐ We'll take the check, please.
☐ We're ready to order.
☐ No, thanks. We'll take the check, please.
☐ Do you accept credit cards?
☐ Excuse me!

C ▷ **PAIR WORK.** Imagine you're in a restaurant. Practice asking and answering the questions. Write the answers. Then reverse roles and do it again.

Your questions   **Your partner's answers**

1. What do you feel like eating for an appetizer?  _____

2. What do you want for a main course? _____

3. What would you like for a beverage? _____

4. How about a dessert? What are you in the mood for? _____

ROLE PLAY. Form groups of diners and servers at tables. Practice discussing the menu and ordering and paying for food.

Land and Sea

All Entrées include
Bread • Pasta or Salad • Vegetable
Coffee or Tea

APPETIZERS
Fried clams • Mini vegetable pies (2) • Shrimp salad

SOUP
French onion • Beef vegetable • Spicy fish

ENTRÉES
Steak • Chicken and rice • Mixed grilled seafood

Children's menu available

DESSERTS
Chocolate cake • Carrot cake

NEED HELP?   Here's language you already know:

Discuss food

What do you feel like eating?
I'm in the mood for ____.
There's ____ on the menu.
The ____ sound(s) delicious!
What about ____?

Serve food

Are you ready to order?
Do you need more time?
That comes with ____.
Would you like ____?
Anything to drink?
And to drink?
And for your main course /
   dessert / beverage?

Order food

Excuse me!
I'm / We're ready.
I'd like to start with ____.
I think I'll have ____.
And then I'll have ____.
Does that come with ____?
What kind of ____ is there?

Pay for food

I'll / We'll take the check,
   please.
Is the tip included?
Do you accept credit
   cards?

FREE PRACTICE

4 Discuss Food and Health

A   🎧 **VOCABULARY.   Food and health.   Listen and practice.**

healthy (or healthful)   good for your body
> Take care of your body! Choose foods that are healthy.

fatty   containing a lot of fat or oil
> Some fatty foods are meat, fried foods, and cheese.

a portion   the amount of a food that you eat at one time
> Eat at least five portions of fruit and vegetables every day.

a meal   breakfast, lunch, or dinner
> Many people eat three meals a day.

a snack   food you eat between meals
> Raw vegetables are a healthy low-calorie snack, but
> many people prefer high-fat snacks like potato chips and nuts.

in moderation   not too much
> Eat sweets in moderation. Small portions are better.

"Veggies"

B   **READING WARM-UP.   Is eating healthy food important to you?**

C   🎧 **READING.   Read the tips from the nutrition website. Which tip do you think is the most important?**

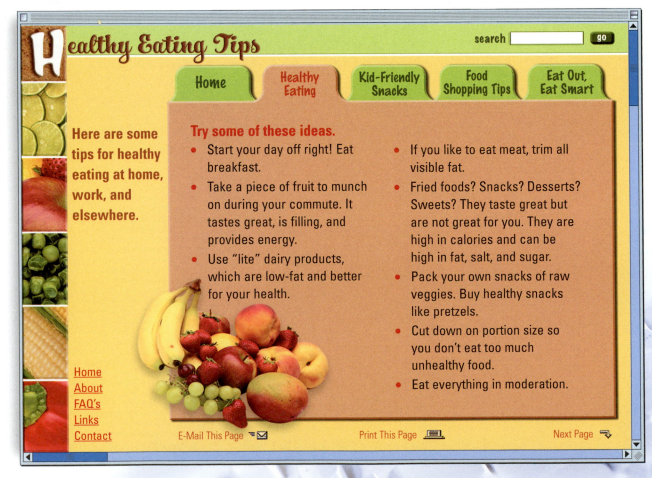

Healthy Eating Tips

search [   ] [go]

| Home | Healthy Eating | Kid-Friendly Snacks | Food Shopping Tips | Eat Out, Eat Smart |

Here are some tips for healthy eating at home, work, and elsewhere.

Try some of these ideas.

- Start your day off right! Eat breakfast.
- Take a piece of fruit to munch on during your commute. It tastes great, is filling, and provides energy.
- Use "lite" dairy products, which are low-fat and better for your health.

- If you like to eat meat, trim all visible fat.
- Fried foods? Snacks? Desserts? Sweets? They taste great but are not great for you. They are high in calories and can be high in fat, salt, and sugar.
- Pack your own snacks of raw veggies. Buy healthy snacks like pretzels.
- Cut down on portion size so you don't eat too much unhealthy food.
- Eat everything in moderation.

Home
About
FAQ's
Links
Contact

E-Mail This Page ✉   Print This Page 🖨   Next Page ➦

SOURCE: http://www.nlm.nih.gov/medlineplus/

UNDERSTANDING MEANING FROM CONTEXT. Use each sentence to help you understand the meaning of each underlined word or phrase.

1. Take a piece of fruit to <u>munch on</u> during your commute.
   - ☐ eat
   - ☐ buy

2. If you like to eat meat, <u>trim</u> all visible fat.
   - ☐ eat
   - ☐ cut off

3. Use "<u>lite</u>" dairy products which are low-fat and better for your health.
   - ☐ fatty
   - ☐ not fatty

4. <u>Cut down on portion size</u> so you don't eat too much unhealthy food.
   - ☐ Eat larger portions
   - ☐ Eat smaller portions

TOP NOTCH
INTERACTION • *What's Good?*

STEP 1.   PAIR WORK. Together write a check mark ✔ next to the foods you think are healthy. Write an ✗ next to the foods you think are not healthy. Do you agree or disagree?

_____ rice   _____ french fries   _____ peppers and garlic   _____ ice cream

_____ nuts and chips   _____ chicken   _____ salad   _____ pasta with sauce

STEP 2.   On the notepad, classify the foods from the pictures.

spicy: *peppers and garlic*

fatty:

salty:

sweet:

STEP 3.   DISCUSSION.   What kind of food do you like? Do you eat healthy foods? What do you eat in moderation? Discuss with your classmates.

UNIT 5
CHECKPOINT

A 🎧 **LISTENING COMPREHENSION.** Listen critically to the conversations. Are they in a restaurant or at home? Check ☑ the boxes.

	Restaurant	Home
1.	☐	☐
2.	☐	☐
3.	☐	☐
4.	☐	☐

B Classify foods. Complete the chart with some foods in each category.

Fruit	Vegetables	Meat	Dairy products	Seafood	Grains

C Write four questions you can ask a waiter or a waitress.

1. _____?
2. _____?
3. _____?
4. _____?

D Complete with a form of <u>there is</u> or <u>there are</u>.

1. _____ too much pepper in the soup.

2. I hope _____ not too much sugar in the cake. Sugar isn't good for you.

3. I'm looking for a good restaurant. _____ any restaurants near you?

4. _____ any low-fat desserts on the menu?

5. _____ an inexpensive restaurant nearby?

6. You should eat some fruit. _____ some oranges on the kitchen table.

7. _____ enough cheese in the fridge for two sandwiches?

8. I'm in the mood for soup. What kind of soup _____ on the menu?

🎧 *TOP NOTCH* SONG
"The World Café"
Lyrics on last book page.

TOP NOTCH PROJECT
• In groups, choose traditional dishes to describe to a visitor to this country.
• Practice describing the dishes and their ingredients, and how they taste.

TOP NOTCH WEBSITE
For Unit 5 online activities, visit the *Top Notch* Companion Website at www.longman.com/topnotch.

E **WRITING.** On a separate piece of paper, write information about food in this country for the readers of a travel newsletter.

UNIT WRAP-UP

- **Vocabulary.** Look at the pictures. Then close your book and write the names of all the foods you remember.

- **Grammar.** Write statements with <u>there is</u>/<u>there are</u> for the foods.

- **Social language.** Create conversations for the people.

- **Writing.** Write a story about the family.

LATER

✔ **Now I can ...**

☐ discuss what to eat.
☐ make food choices.
☐ order and pay for a meal.
☐ discuss food and health.

63

Staying in Shape

UNIT GOALS

1 Plan an activity with someone
2 Talk about daily routines
3 Discuss exercise and diet
4 Describe your typical day

A TOPIC PREVIEW. Look at the graphs. Which activities do you do regularly?

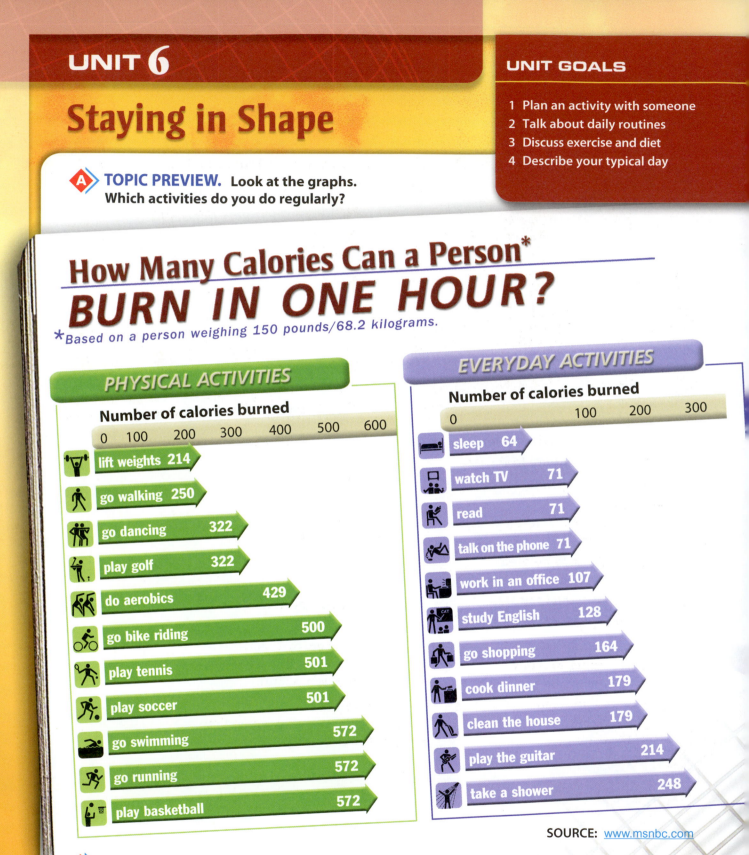

How Many Calories Can a Person*
BURN IN ONE HOUR?
*Based on a person weighing 150 pounds/68.2 kilograms.

PHYSICAL ACTIVITIES

Number of calories burned

lift weights	214
go walking	250
go dancing	322
play golf	322
do aerobics	429
go bike riding	500
play tennis	501
play soccer	501
go swimming	572
go running	572
play basketball	572

EVERYDAY ACTIVITIES

Number of calories burned

sleep	64
watch TV	71
read	71
talk on the phone	71
work in an office	107
study English	128
go shopping	164
cook dinner	179
clean the house	179
play the guitar	214
take a shower	248

SOURCE: www.msnbc.com

B VOCABULARY. Activities. Listen and practice.

C DISCUSSION. Do you burn a lot of calories every day? Who in your class burns more than 1500 calories a day?

🎧 SOUND BITES. Read along silently as you listen to a natural conversation.

SUE: Hey, Jane! Where are you off to?

JANE: I'm on my way to the park.

SUE: You play tennis? How often?

JANE: Just about every weekend. Do you want to play together sometime?

SUE: That would be great.

SUE: What about your husband? Does he play?

JANE: Ed? No way. He's a couch potato.

SUE: Too bad. My husband's crazy about tennis.

E ▶ UNDERSTANDING MEANING FROM CONTEXT. Use the conversation to help you choose the correct response.

1. "Where are you off to?"
   ☐ I'm going to work.
   ☐ I play tennis.

2. "Do you lift weights?"
   ☐ No kidding.
   ☐ No way.

3. "Does your daughter play golf?"
   ☐ Yes. She's crazy about golf.
   ☐ Yes. She's a couch potato.

4. "How often do you play tennis?"
   ☐ Well, let's play together some time.
   ☐ I don't. I'm a couch potato.

WHAT ABOUT YOU?

Write about your activities.

Every day	Every weekend	Once a week	Once in a while	Never
I study English.				

1 Plan an Activity with Someone

🎧 CONVERSATION MODEL Read and listen.

A: Hey, Paul. Why don't we play basketball sometime?
B: Great idea. When's good for you?
A: Tomorrow at three?
B: Sorry, I can't. I have to meet my sister at the airport.
A: How about Wednesday at five?
B: That sounds great.

🎧 **Rhythm and intonation practice**

A ▶ GRAMMAR. Can and have to

can

Use can + the base form of a verb for ability or possibility.

  I **can speak** English, but I **can't speak** Italian.
  I **can't play** golf today. I'm too busy.

Yes / no questions

  Can you **come** for dinner this evening?

Short answers

  Yes, I can. / No, I can't.

can't = { can not
           cannot

---

have to

Use have to + the base form of a verb for obligation.

  I can't go running tomorrow. I **have to meet** my cousin after class.
  She can't come for dinner. She **has to work** late.
  Dave can sleep late. He **doesn't have to go** to work.
  Relax! You **don't have to drive** to the airport until 10:00.

Yes / no questions

  Do you **have to work** tomorrow?
  Does she **have to go** to school today?

Short answers

  Yes, I do. / No, I don't.
  Yes, she does. / No, she doesn't.

don't = do not
doesn't = does no[t]

GRAMMAR BOOSTER

PAGES G10–G12
For more . . .

B ▶ Complete the sentences with can or have to.

1. Vicky _____ for dinner tonight. She _____ a report for her boss.
   _{not / come}   _{finish}

2. I _____ you at 6:00. I _____ late tonight.
   _{meet}   _{not / work}

3. My brother _____ soccer today. He _____ to the doctor.
   _{not / play}   _{go}

4. I want to see a movie, but I have an exam tomorrow. I _____ tonight.
   _{study}

5. _____ Nick _____ golf with us next Wednesday?
   _{play}

C 🎧 **PRONUNCIATION.** <u>Can</u> / <u>can't</u>. **Listen to the pronunciation and stress of <u>can</u> and <u>can't</u> in sentences. Then listen again and repeat.**

/kən/

•

I can **call** you tomorrow.

/kænt/

•

I **can't** call you tomorrow.

🎧 **Now listen carefully and check <u>can</u> or <u>can't</u>. Then listen again and repeat.**

1. ☐ can ☐ can't
2. ☐ can ☐ can't
3. ☐ can ☐ can't

4. ☐ can ☐ can't
5. ☐ can ☐ can't
6. ☐ can ☐ can't

D **PAIR WORK.** **Write three invitations using <u>can</u>. Then read your partner's invitations and write excuses.**

Can you go swimming tomorrow?

Sorry, I can't. I have to work.

CONVERSATION PAIR WORK

Write your schedule for this weekend in the daily planner.

GROUP WORK. **Talk to at least three different classmates. Plan an activity together this weekend. Use your daily planner.**

A: _____. Why don't we _____ sometime?

B: Great idea. When's good for you?

A: _____?

B: _____ ...

Continue the conversation in your <u>own</u> way.

	FRIDAY	SATURDAY	SUNDAY
9:00	go running	visit Mom	

Daily Planner

	FRIDAY	SATURDAY	SUNDAY
9:00			
11:00			
1:00			
3:00			
5:00			
7:00			

LESSON 2

Talk about Daily Routines

🎧 **CONVERSATION MODEL** Read and listen.

A: Janet! What are <u>you</u> doing here?

B: Hi, Lisa. I always go to the gym on Saturday morning. You too?

A: Actually, I usually go in the evening. But not today.

B: How come?

A: I'm going to the theater tonight.

B: Well, have a great time.

🎧 **Rhythm and intonation practice**

A ▶ **GRAMMAR.** The simple present tense and the present continuous

The simple present tense

Use the simple present tense to describe frequency, habits, and routines.

How often **do** you **play** basketball?	I **play** basketball at least once a week.
When **does** Paula **do** aerobics?	She **does** aerobics on Tuesdays.
When **do** you usually **go** to the gym?	I usually **go** in the evening.

The present continuous

Use the present continuous for actions in progress now or for future plans.

She**'s talking** on the phone.   Paul and Judy **are going** running tomorrow.

Don't use the present continuous with frequency adverbs.
    Don't say: ~~She's usually talking on the phone.~~
Don't use the present continuous with <u>have</u>, <u>want</u>, <u>need</u>, or <u>like</u>.
    Don't say: ~~She's liking the gym.~~

Frequency adverbs
100%   always *1100*
    almost always *96*
    usually / often *80*
    sometimes *60 70*
0%   hardly ever *40 – 20*
    never *– 0 –*

GRAMMAR BOOSTER

PAGES G12–G13
For more . . .

B ▶ Complete the sentences. Use the simple present tense or the present continuous.

1. How often _____ running?
    you / go

2. I'm sorry. _____ right now.
    Paul / study

3. _____ to the track this afternoon.
    I / go

4. _____ weights three times a week.
    I / lift

5. _____ lunch. Can he call you back?
    Tim / cook

6. How often _____ the guitar?
    you / play

7. _____ tennis every day.
    I / play

C. 🎧 VOCABULARY. Places for physical activities. Listen and practice.

a park

a gym

a track

a pool

an athletic field

a golf course

a tennis court

D. 🎧 LISTENING COMPREHENSION. Listen to each conversation. Match the conversation with the place.

___f___ 1.   **a.** a park

_____ 2.   **b.** a gym

_____ 3.   **c.** a track

_____ 4.   **d.** a pool

_____ 5.   **e.** an athletic field

_____ 6.   **f.** a golf course

_____ 7.   **g.** a tennis court

CONVERSATION PAIR WORK

Talk about daily routines. Use the guide, or create a new conversation.

A: _____ ! What are <u>you</u> doing here?

B: Hi, _____ . I always _____ on _____ .
You too?

A: Actually, I usually _____ . But not today.

B: How come?

A: _____ …

Continue the conversation in your <u>own</u> way.

What are you doing here?

I always go skydiving on Mondays!

3

Discuss Exercise and Diet

A ⌾ VOCABULARY. Talking about health habits. Listen and practice.

| be in shape | be out of shape | eat junk food | avoid sweets | have a sweet tooth |

B Practice the new vocabulary. Complete each statement.

1. I hardly ever exercise, and I usually don't feel healthy. I'm really _____.
   a. in great shape   b. out of shape   c. a sweet tooth

2. I generally try to eat healthy foods. I avoid _____.
   a. fatty foods   b. vegetables   c. fruits

3. My son has a real sweet tooth. He loves _____.
   a. fish   b. candy   c. meat

C ⌾ LISTENING COMPREHENSION. Listen to people talk about their health habits. Then listen again and check the statements that are true.

1. Juan Reyneri:
- ☐ generally eats small meals.
- ☐ generally eats large meals.
- ☐ usually drinks soft drinks.
- ☐ usually drinks a lot of water.
- ☐ exercises regularly.
- ☐ doesn't exercise regularly.

2. Naomi Sato:
- ☐ exercises regularly.
- ☐ doesn't exercise regularly.
- ☐ eats fish once a week.
- ☐ hardly ever eats fish.
- ☐ eats fruits and vegetables every day.
- ☐ hardly ever eats fruits and vegetables.

3. Matt Lemke:
- ☐ exercises regularly.
- ☐ doesn't exercise regularly.
- ☐ generally avoids fatty foods.
- ☐ doesn't avoid fatty foods.
- ☐ always drinks a lot of water.
- ☐ always drinks soft drinks.

D ⌾ PRONUNCIATION. Third-person singular -s. Listen. Then repeat.

/s/	/z/	/ɪz/
sleeps	goes	watches
eats	plays	exercises
works	avoids	munches

STEP 1. Take the health survey.

TOP NOTCH HEALTH SURVEY

Check the statements that are true for you.
Then add up your total score.

1. ☐ **a.** I exercise regularly.
   ☐ **b.** I don't have time to exercise regularly.
   ☐ **c.** I don't want to exercise regularly.

2. ☐ **a.** I always get enough sleep.
   ☐ **b.** I sometimes don't get enough sleep.
   ☐ **c.** I never get enough sleep.

3. ☐ **a.** I always eat vegetables.
   ☐ **b.** I sometimes eat vegetables.
   ☐ **c.** I never eat vegetables.

4. ☐ **a.** I avoid fatty foods.
   ☐ **b.** I sometimes eat fatty foods.
   ☐ **c.** I eat lots of fatty foods.

5. ☐ **a.** I hardly ever eat sweets.
   ☐ **b.** I sometimes eat sweets.
   ☐ **c.** I have a sweet tooth.

Score
Each **a** answer = 10 points.
Each **b** answer = 5 points.
Each **c** answer = 0 points.

Total points: ☐

40–50 points =
You're in terrific shape!

30–35 points =
Not bad. Keep it up!

20–25 points =
Come on. Try harder!

0–15 points =
You're a couch potato!

STEP 2. PAIR WORK. Compare your survey answers and scores. Then compare your exercise and diet habits.

> ❝ Do you exercise at home? How often? ❞

STEP 3. PAIR WORK. Walk around your classroom and ask questions. Write your classmates' names on the chart.

Find someone who ...	Name	
1. eats a lot of junk food.	Yes Mata	
2. lifts weights regularly.		
3. doesn't have time to exercise.		
4. exercises at home.		
5. never eats sweets.		
6. doesn't get enough sleep every night.		
7. goes running regularly.		

STEP 4. GROUP WORK. Tell your class about some of your classmates.

> ❝ Frank exercises at home every day. ❞

71

FREE PRACTICE

4 Describe Your Typical Day

LESSON

A ▶ **READING WARM-UP.** Look at the photo. What do you think is the relationship between the two women? What do you think they are doing?

B ▶ 🎧 **READING.** Read the article about Brooke Ellison. How is her day different from yours?

With her mother's help, Brooke Ellison remains active

In June 2000, Brooke Ellison graduated from Harvard University. And now she is continuing her studies as a full-time graduate student. Brooke is a quadriplegic—she can't move her arms or legs. She spends all her time in a wheelchair, and she can't breathe without a special machine. A terrible accident at the age of 11 changed her life—she was hit by a car on her way home from school. But she stays active every day.

On a typical morning, it takes most people about a half hour to get up, get dressed, and have breakfast. For Brooke, it usually takes about four hours. Her mother, Jean, wakes her early in the morning and exercises her arms and legs. Then she gives her a bath, combs her hair, and brushes her teeth. After that, she dresses her and lifts her into her wheelchair. By late morning, Brooke is ready for breakfast. In the afternoon, Brooke goes to her classes and listens carefully. Her mother goes to classes with her and takes notes. For a lot of activities, such as using a calculator, Brooke uses her mouth, instead of her hands and legs. She can move her wheelchair by blowing into a tube.

At night, she does her homework and reads her e-mail, and she often phones her brother or sister to talk. To use a computer, she uses her voice—she tells the computer what to do. At about 8:00, she gets ready for bed—it usually takes about two hours. Her mother undresses her, bathes her, and exercises her arms and legs again.

When she can, Brooke gives speeches to young people. She tells them about her life and teaches them to always be active.

SOURCES: *Miracles Happen,* Brooke and Jean Ellison, 2001, Hyperion and *The Brooke Ellison Story,* directed by Christopher Reeve, 2004

C ▶ **Read the article again.** Complete each statement with <u>can</u>, <u>can't</u>, or <u>has to</u>.

Brooke Ellison:

1. _**can't**_ walk.
2. _____ use a wheelchair.
3. _____ breathe without a special machine.
4. _____ get up early every day.
5. _____ use a computer.
6. _____ use a calculator.
7. _____ use her hands.
8. _____ read her e-mail.

D Write what Brooke and Jean Ellison do each day.

In the morning: _Brooke gets up early. Jean combs her hair._
_____
_____

In the afternoon: _____
_____
_____

In the evening: _____
_____
_____

INTERACTION • *What About You?*

STEP 1. **Answer the questions about your typical day.**

1. What time do you usually get up? _____.
2. What do you do next? _____.
3. Do you usually eat breakfast? _____.
4. When do you usually have lunch? _____.
5. What do you do in the evening? _____.
6. What time do you go to bed? _____.

STEP 2. **PAIR WORK. Interview a partner about his or her activities on a typical day. Use some or all of the questions in Step 1. Take notes on the notepad.**

In the morning	In the afternoon	In the evening

STEP 3. DISCUSSION. Tell your class about your partner's typical day.

STEP 4. WRITING. Write an article about your partner's typical day.

In the morning, Nina usually gets up early and goes running. After that, she eats breakfast. She usually has cereal and juice. After breakfast...

73

FREE PRACTICE

A 🎧 **LISTENING COMPREHENSION.** Listen carefully. Check ☑ the box to complete each statement. Then listen again to check your work.

1. She ___ eats breakfast. ☐ usually ☑ never ☐ almost always
2. Tony ___ goes swimming on Mondays. ☑ usually ☐ never ☐ hardly ever
3. He ___ eats healthy food. ☐ never ☑ almost always ☐ hardly ever
4. She goes running ___. ☑ daily ☐ once in a while ☐ three times a week

B What physical activities can you do in each of these places? Write sentences.

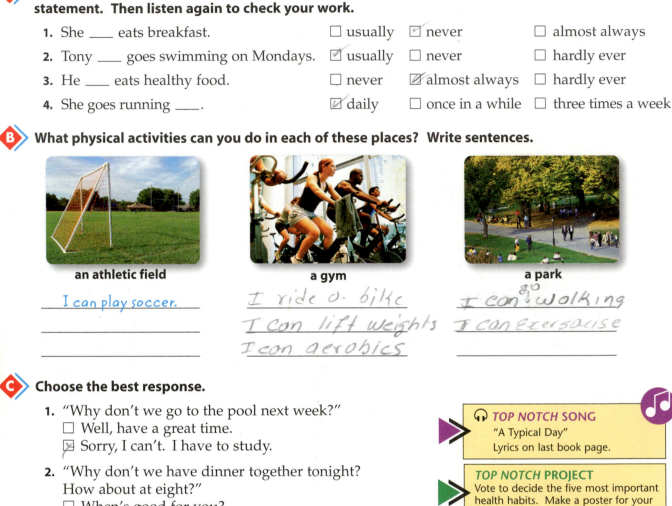

an athletic field

I can play soccer.
___
___

a gym

I ride a bike
I can lift weights
I can aerobics

a park

I can go walking
I can exersaise
___

C Choose the best response.

1. "Why don't we go to the pool next week?"
   ☐ Well, have a great time.
   ☑ Sorry, I can't. I have to study.

2. "Why don't we have dinner together tonight? How about at eight?"
   ☐ When's good for you?
   ☑ Sure. Sounds great.

3. "What are you doing here?"
   ☐ Sorry, I can't.
   ☑ I always have lunch here on Saturdays.

🎧 **TOP NOTCH SONG**
"A Typical Day"
Lyrics on last book page.

TOP NOTCH PROJECT
Vote to decide the five most important health habits. Make a poster for your class.

TOP NOTCH WEBSITE
For Unit 6 online activities, visit the *Top Notch* Companion Website at www.longman.com/topnotch.

D Answer the questions with real information.

1. How often do you go to your English class? **YOU** I can everey dey .
2. Are you going to your English class tomorrow? **YOU** I will .
3. What do you usually do on weekends? **YOU** Waches tv. .
4. What are you doing this weekend? **YOU** I an going to visit my friend

E **WRITING.** Write about **your** typical day.

Every morning, I get up at 6:30. I usually take a shower and ...

UNIT WRAP-UP

- **Vocabulary and grammar.** Talk about how often you do the activities in the picture.
- **Social language.** Create a conversation for the two men.
- **Writing.** Write about the people. *A woman is cooking.*

Mini Golf

Blue Moon Café

Total Fitness

✓ *Now I can ...*

☐ plan an activity with someone.
☐ talk about daily routines.
☐ discuss exercise and diet.
☐ describe my typical day.

Finding Something to Wear

UNIT GOALS

1 Shop for clothes
2 Pay for clothes
3 Give and get directions in a store
4 Discuss culturally appropriate dress

A TOPIC PREVIEW. Look at the store website. What department would <u>you</u> click on?

Shop at Home Online Department Store

Large selection of fine brand-name clothes FOR THE WHOLE FAMILY!

shop at home ONLINE DEPARTMENT STORE

"... Just click your mouse.
Stay in your house."®

SIGN IN | REGISTER | MY ACCOUNT | CUSTOMER SERVICE | CHECKOUT | VIEW CART

DEPARTMENTS

Women's

Men's

Teens'

Kids'

Athletic Wear

Outerwear
(coats and jackets)

Sleepwear

Lingerie

Hosiery

Shoes

Bags and
Accessories

SEARCH [____] GO

| SPECIALS | OUTERWEAR | HOSIERY | SLEEPWEAR | BAGS and ACCESSORIES | ATHLETIC WEAR |

OUTERWEAR SALE
SAVE 30–50% on <u>jackets</u>

Arctic brand unisex windbreaker

HOSIERY CLEARANCE!

men's socks   women's tights

THIS WEEK'S SPECIALS
Click on items for special prices and other details.

ALL SLEEPWEAR, UNDERWEAR, AND LINGERIE ON SALE!

men's boxers   men's pajamas   women's nightgowns   bathrobes

SAVE 40–50% on all
BAGS and ACCESSORIES

leather bags   belts

100+ brands all on sale!
ATHLETIC WEAR

running shoes   shorts   sweatpants

HOME | OTHER PRODUCTS & SERVICES | GIFT CARDS | CATALOGS | ABOUT US | CONTACT US

B DISCUSSION. Where do you shop for clothes? Do you ever shop online?

C 🎧 **SOUND BITES.** Read along silently as you listen to a natural conversation.

SHOPPER: Excuse me. How much is that V-neck?

CLERK: This red one? It's $55.

SHOPPER: That's not too bad. And it's really nice.

SHOPPER: Do you have it in a larger size?

CLERK: Here you go. This one's a medium. Would you like to try it on?

SHOPPER: No, thanks. It's for my sister. Would you be nice enough to gift wrap it for me?

CLERK: Of course!

D Read the conversation carefully and check ☑ the statements that are true. Then explain your answers.

☐ **1.** The clerk asks about the price.
☐ **2.** The first sweater is the right size.
☐ **3.** The sweater is a gift.
☐ **4.** The shopper buys the sweater.

E **UNDERSTANDING MEANING FROM CONTEXT.** Complete the statements.

1. When the shopper says, "Excuse me," she means _____.
a. Can you help me?   **b.** I don't understand.

2. When the shopper says, "That's not too bad," she means _____.
a. The sweater is nice.   **b.** The price is not too high.

3. When the clerk says, "Here you go," she means _____.
a. Here's a cheaper one.   **b.** Here's a larger one.

WHAT ABOUT **YOU?**

What's important to you when you choose a place to shop for clothes?
Complete the chart.

	Not important	Important	Very important
Prices	○	○	○
Brands	○	○	○
Selection	○	○	○
Service	○	○	○

PAIR WORK. Compare your opinions.

1 *Shop for Clothes*

CONVERSATION MODEL Read and listen.

A: Excuse me. Do you have these gloves in a larger size?

B: No, I'm sorry. We don't.

A: That's too bad.

B: But we have a larger pair in brown. See if they are better.

A: Yes, they're fine. Thanks.

Rhythm and intonation practice

A GRAMMAR. Comparative adjectives

small → small**er**	large → larg**er**	heavy → heav**ier**	big → big**ger**
cheap → cheap**er**	loose → loos**er**	pretty → prett**ier**	hot → hot**ter**

Irregular forms
good → better
bad → worse

Use comparative adjectives to compare two people, places, or things.

Do you have these pants in a **larger** size? This pair is too tight.

Use more or less with adjectives that have two or more syllables and don't end in -y.

Do you have a **more comfortable** pair of shoes?
Let's look for a **less expensive** suit.

Use than after the adjective when you compare two items.

Some people say that black is more flattering **than** white, but white looks better on me.

GRAMMAR BOOSTER

PAGES G13–G14
For more . . .

B Complete each conversation with comparative adjectives. Use **than** if necessary.

1. **A:** I just love these gloves, but I wish they were ___warmer___ .
   _{warm}

   B: What about these? They look great, and they're much _less expensive_
   _{expensive}

2. **A:** Don't take those pajamas to Hawaii! It's hot there. Take something _lighter_ .
   _{light}

   B: Good idea.

3. **A:** What do you think of this red dress?

   B: Beautiful. It's _Prettier_ the black one. And _cheaper_ , too.
   _{pretty}   _{cheap}

4. **A:** Excuse me. Do these pants come in a _longer_ length? These are too short.
   _{long}

   B: Let me see if I can find you something _better_ .
   _{good}

C 🎧 VOCABULARY. Clothing described as "pairs." Listen and practice.

(a pair of) gloves

(a pair of) pajamas

(a pair of) socks

(a pair of) panties

(a pair of) boxers
(a pair of) briefs

(a pair of) pantyhose
(a pair of) tights

(a pair of) pants
(a pair of) shorts

D 🎧 LISTENING COMPREHENSION. Circle the clothing discussed in each conversation.

1. stockings   gloves
2. boxers   pajamas
3. tights   gloves
4. pajamas   boxers
5. pantyhose   panties

CONVERSATION PAIR WORK

Role-play shopping for clothes. Start like this:

Excuse me.
Do you have _____?

Continue the conversation in your own way . . .

Ideas

in a smaller size
in a larger size
in another color
in [black]
in size [34]

CONTROLLED PRACTICE

Pay for Clothes

🎧 CONVERSATION MODEL Read and listen.

A: I'll take the loafers.

B: Certainly. How would you like to pay for them?

A: Excuse me?

B: Cash or charge?

A: Charge, please. And could you gift wrap them for me?

B: Absolutely.

🎧 **Rhythm and intonation practice**

A 🎧 **VOCABULARY.** Types of clothing and shoes. **Listen and practice.**

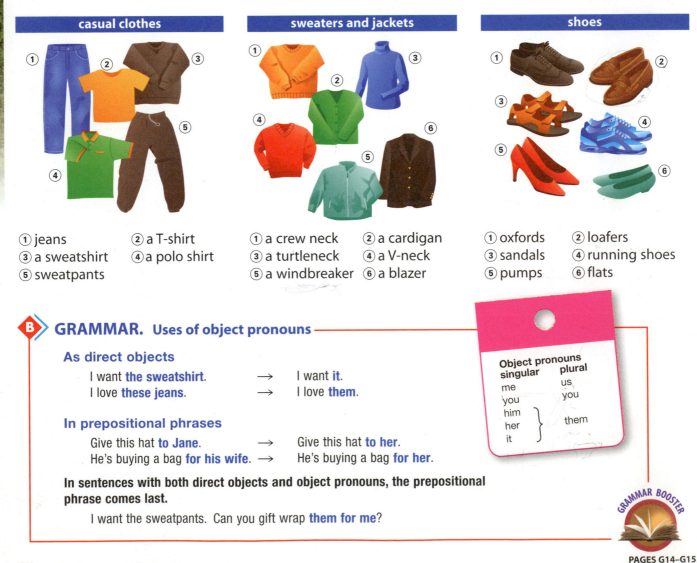

casual clothes

① jeans ② a T-shirt
③ a sweatshirt ④ a polo shirt
⑤ sweatpants

sweaters and jackets

① a crew neck ② a cardigan
③ a turtleneck ④ a V-neck
⑤ a windbreaker ⑥ a blazer

shoes

① oxfords ② loafers
③ sandals ④ running shoes
⑤ pumps ⑥ flats

B **GRAMMAR.** Uses of object pronouns

As direct objects

I want **the sweatshirt**. → I want **it**.
I love **these jeans**. → I love **them**.

In prepositional phrases

Give this hat **to Jane**. → Give this hat **to her**.
He's buying a bag **for his wife**. → He's buying a bag **for her**.

In sentences with both direct objects and object pronouns, the prepositional phrase comes last.

I want the sweatpants. Can you gift wrap **them for me**?

Object pronouns	
singular	**plural**
me	us
you	you
him	
her	} them
it	

GRAMMAR BOOSTER

PAGES G14–G15
For more . . .

C ▷ Underline the direct object in each sentence. Then rewrite the sentence, replacing the direct object with an object pronoun.

1. They bought <u>the green sweatpants</u>.
    _They bought them_____.

2. I love <u>these windbreakers</u>.
    _I love them_____.

3. I'm buying <u>the crew neck</u>.
    _I'm buying it_____.

4. Did you see <u>the blue polo shirts</u>?
    _Did you see it_____?

5. I don't need <u>the cardigan</u>.
    _I don't need it_____.

6. Do you still have <u>that great pair of flats</u>?
    _Do you still have _____?

7. They gave <u>the old jackets</u> to us.
    _they gave them to us_____.

D ▷ Write the words and phrases in the correct order.

1. I / it / for her / am buying
    _____.

2. They / them / for us / are getting
    _____.

3. Please / it / to me / give
    _____.

4. for my son-in-law / I / them / need
    _____.

5. it / He / is gift wrapping / for me
    _____.

CONVERSATION
PAIR WORK

Role-play paying for clothes. Use the guide, or create a new conversation.

A: I'll take the _____.
B: _____. How would you like to pay for _____?
A: Excuse me?
B: Cash or charge?
A: _____, please. And could you gift wrap _____ for me?
B: _____.

CONTROLLED PRACTICE

81

Give and Get Directions in a Store

A 🎧 **VOCABULARY.** Locations and directions. Listen and practice.

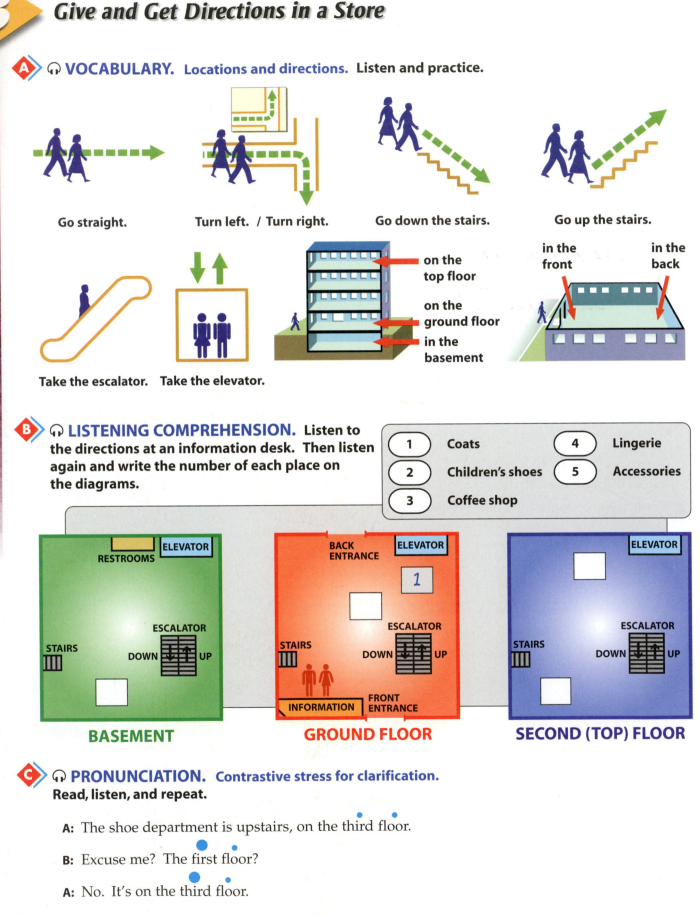

Go straight.

Turn left. / Turn right.

Go down the stairs.

Go up the stairs.

Take the escalator.   Take the elevator.

on the top floor

on the ground floor

in the basement

in the front   in the back

B 🎧 **LISTENING COMPREHENSION.** Listen to the directions at an information desk. Then listen again and write the number of each place on the diagrams.

1	Coats	4	Lingerie
2	Children's shoes	5	Accessories
3	Coffee shop		

BASEMENT

RESTROOMS   ELEVATOR

STAIRS

ESCALATOR   DOWN   UP

GROUND FLOOR

BACK ENTRANCE   ELEVATOR

1

STAIRS

ESCALATOR   DOWN   UP

INFORMATION   FRONT ENTRANCE

SECOND (TOP) FLOOR

ELEVATOR

STAIRS

ESCALATOR   DOWN   UP

C 🎧 **PRONUNCIATION.** Contrastive stress for clarification. Read, listen, and repeat.

A: The shoe department is upstairs, on the third floor.

B: Excuse me? The first floor?

A: No. It's on the third floor.

TOP NOTCH INTERACTION

STEP 1. On the notepad, write things you can find in each department.

Men's:	Lingerie:
Women's:	Electronics:
Shoes:	Appliances:

STEP 2. PAIR WORK. Look at the department store floor plan and store directory. Role-play conversations between a shopper and an information clerk. Use the items on the notepad.

"Excuse me. Where are the ...?"

STORE DIRECTORY

Bags and Accessories	Ground Floor
Electronics	Basement
Hosiery	Ground Floor
Lingerie	Ground Floor
Men's Athleticwear	2
Men's Casual	2
Men's Outerwear	2
Men's Shoes	2
Men's Sleepwear	2
Men's Underwear	2
Photo Studio	Basement
Restaurant	Basement
Small Appliances	Basement
Women's Casual	Ground Floor
Women's Shoes	Ground Floor

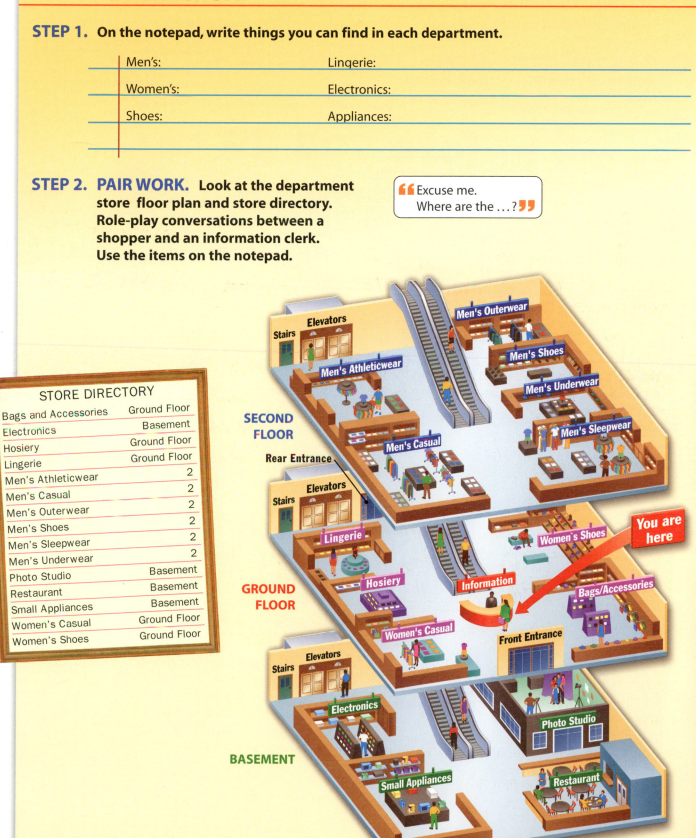

SECOND FLOOR

GROUND FLOOR

BASEMENT

4 Discuss Culturally Appropriate Dress

A ▶ **READING WARM-UP.** What do you wear when the weather is warm? —when you want to look informal? —when you need to look more formal?

B ▶ 🎧 **READING.** Read about clothing do's and don'ts for travelers. Then explain why this information is helpful.

Know before you go . . .

Every culture has unwritten "rules" about appropriate and inappropriate dress. Some cultures have a liberal attitude about clothing, while other cultures are more conservative. Read about some clothing do's and don'ts for three popular travel destinations around the world.

Holland
Holland has a northern climate, so depending on the time of year you're visiting, pack lighter or heavier clothes. One thing people notice about Holland is the way young people dress. Their dress code is "anything goes," so it's not unusual to see some pretty wild clothes there!

Thailand
If you're visiting beautiful Thailand from May to September, pack for the heat. Thailand is generally conservative when it comes to clothing, but at Thailand's magnificent temples, the rules about clothing, and especially shoes, are very strict. If your shoes are too open, they are considered disrespectful, and you will have to change to more modest ones. So be prepared with light but modest clothing and shoes for your Thailand trip.

a Thai temple

an Egyptian mosque

Egypt
Summertime is hot in Egypt, so pack light clothing. But be sure to bring warm-weather clothing that is also modest. If you visit a mosque, shorts are definitely out of the question, for both men and women. In mosques, women should wear longer skirts and a head covering, usually a scarf. And the upper part of their arms should be covered with sleeves. For touring other wonderful sights and historical places, casual, comfortable clothing is fine for both men and women.

SOURCE: *Rough Guide* and *Berlitz* travel guides

C **DISCUSSION.** Rate the dress code for each country. Then explain each rating you made.

	conservative		liberal		"anything goes!"
Egypt	✓	○	○	○	○
Holland	○	○	○	○	○
Thailand	○	○	○	○	○
This country	○	○	○	○	○

D **PAIR WORK.** Plan your clothes for a July visit to one of the following places.

- an Egyptian mosque
- the pyramids in Egypt
- a casual restaurant in Holland
- a Thai temple

TOP NOTCH
INTERACTION • Do's and Don'ts

STEP 1. Take the opinion survey.

What's your personal dress code?

Circle "agree" or "disagree" for each statement about clothing.

It's OK to wear shorts on the street.	agree	disagree
It's OK for men to wear shorts on the street, but not for women.	agree	disagree
It's essential for men to wear a tie in the office.	agree	disagree
It's OK for women to wear pants in the office.	agree	disagree
It's OK for young people to be less conservative in clothing than adults.	agree	disagree
It's essential for women to cover their heads in public.	agree	disagree

How would you rate yourself?

☐ conservative ☐ liberal ☐ "anything goes!"

STEP 2. On the notepad, write some clothing do's and don'ts for visitors to this country.

in offices and formal restaurants:

in casual social settings:

in religious institutions:

STEP 3. **GROUP WORK.** Discuss the do's and don'ts for appropriate dress in this country. Does everyone agree?

FREE PRACTICE

85

A **LISTENING COMPREHENSION.** Listen critically to the conversations about clothes. Infer the name of the **department** where the people are talking.

| Outerwear | Lingerie | Hosiery | Bags and accessories | Shoes |

1. _____ 4. _____

2. _____ 5. _____

3. _____

B **Complete each sentence about clothes with an appropriate word.**

1. Two kinds of men's underwear are boxers and _briefs_.

2. Two kinds of leg coverings for women are pantyhose and _tights_.

3. Sandals are a kind of _shoes_.

4. A windbreaker is a kind of _jacket_.

5. You can't buy just one glove. You have to buy a _pair_.

C **Complete the travel article with the comparative form of each adjective.**

When you travel, think carefully about the clothes you pack. As far as color is concerned, _darker_ colors are
1. dark
usually _more practical_. For _cooler_ destinations, a blazer can
2. practical   3. cool
be _more convenient_ than a windbreaker or cardigan because you can
4. convenient
wear it in _more_ settings such as offices and _more_
5. conservative   6. formal
restaurants. For travel to _hotter_ areas of the world,
7. hot
lighter clothes are _more_ than _heavier_ ones.
8. light   9. comfortable   10. heavy

> **TOP NOTCH PROJECT**
> As a group, write a short entry about this country to the travel guide on page 84. Use your survey, your notepad, and the article as a model.

> **TOP NOTCH WEBSITE**
> For Unit 7 online activities, visit the *Top Notch* Companion Website at www.longman.com/topnotch

D **Unscramble each sentence.**

1. Please / to me / them / show _Please show them to me_.

2. They / to us / are sending / it _they are sending it to us_.

3. When / you / are / to her / it / giving _When are you giving it to her_?

4. with you / Take / it _take it with you._

E **WRITING.** Imagine you are taking a trip to another country. On a separate sheet of paper, write about where you are going and what you are going to pack. Explain why. Talk about the climate and the culture.

UNIT WRAP-UP

- **Vocabulary.** Look at the picture. Then close your book and write the names of the clothing you remember.
- **Social language.** Create conversations for the people. Use the directory.
- **Grammar.** Write comparisons.
  The blazer is more formal than the windbreaker.

BAGS AND ACCESSORIES	1
CHILDREN'S DEPARTMENT	3
ELECTRONICS	3
HAIRDRESSER	4
LINGERIE	1
MEN'S DEPARTMENT	1
PHOTO STUDIO	2
RESTAURANTS	4
SHOES	1
TRAVEL AGENCY	2
WOMEN'S DEPARTMENT	1

INFORMATION DESK

✔ **Now I can . . .**

☐ shop for clothes.
☐ pay for clothes.
☐ give and get directions in a store.
☐ discuss culturally appropriate dress.

Getting Away

UNIT GOALS

1 Greet someone arriving from a trip
2 Talk about how you spent your free time
3 Discuss vacation preferences
4 Tell about your experiences on a trip

A **TOPIC PREVIEW.** Look at the travel ads. Which vacations look good to you? Why?

TRAVEL SPECIALS

10 NIGHT Caribbean Cruise

Departs from / Returns to Miami

Miami
Nassau
Cozumel
Belize City
Grand Cayman

Enjoy snorkeling in **Grand Cayman Island**

Go scuba diving in **Belize**

Play with dolphins in **Nassau**

WHAT'S INCLUDED?

✔ Accommodations 🛏
✔ Meals 🍴
✔ Beverages 🥤
✔ Entertainment 🎵

ITALY in Six Days!

ITALY

You'll savor every minute you spend in romantic Italy!

ROME
Discover the Eternal City! Rome is filled with history and romance.

VENICE
Visit historic St. Mark's Square. And don't miss a gondola voyage on the Grand Canal!

Walt Disney World Resorts®

Disney **MGM STUDIOS**

Magic Kingdom®

Something for everyone in your family!
FOUR different theme parks, **THREE** water parks, shopping, dining, and entertainment.
Choose from over 40 great hotels.

Fly-in African Safari

THE SERENGETI NATIONAL PARK

Africa's most spectacular wildlife experience

YOU'LL NEVER FORGET IT!

Duration:
3 days/2 nights

Type: Safari fly-in

Country: Tanzania

Rates (US$):
Available on request

Activities include:
Birdwatching, wildlife viewing

SOURCE: Adapted from www.celebritycruises.com; www.ilove-italy.com; www.ineedavacation.com; www.go2africa.com

B **DISCUSSION.** In your opinion, which of the vacations are good for people who like:

- nature and wildlife?
- family activities?
- history and culture?
- physical activities?

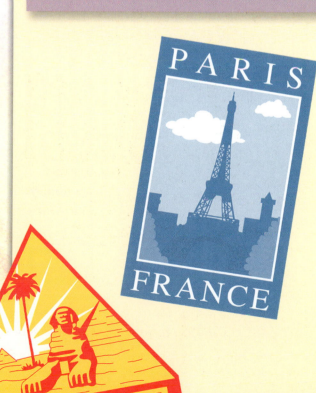 WHAT ABOUT **YOU?**

Answer the questions about <u>your</u> vacations. Check all that apply.

🌐 TRAVEL SURVEY

Where do you usually go on vacation?
- ☐ I visit family.
- ☐ I go to another city.
- ☐ I go to another country.
- ☐ I go to a beach.
- ☐ Other _____

What do you usually do on vacation?
- ☐ I take it easy.
- ☐ I visit museums and go sightseeing.
- ☐ I do a lot of physical activities.
- ☐ I eat at nice restaurants.
- ☐ Other _____

C 🎧 **SOUND BITES.** **Read along silently as you listen to a natural conversation.**

GREG: Hi, Barbara. When did you get back?

BARBARA: Greg! Just yesterday.

GREG: So tell me about your trip.

BARBARA: It was incredible. I had a really great time.

GREG: Good weather?

BARBARA: Not perfect, but generally OK.

GREG: I'll bet the food was great.

BARBARA: Amazing!

D **UNDERSTANDING MEANING FROM CONTEXT.** **Use the conversation to help you choose the correct answer.**

1. When Greg asks, "When did you get back?" he means _____.
   a. When did you come home?
   b. When did you go on your trip?

2. When Barbara says, "It was incredible," she means _____.
   a. It was a good trip.
   b. It wasn't a good trip.

3. When Greg says, "Good weather?" he means _____.
   a. The weather was good.
   b. Was the weather good?

PARIS

FRANCE

CAIRO EGYPT

Greet Someone Arriving from a Trip

🎧 **CONVERSATION MODEL** **Read and listen.**

A: So, how was the flight?

B: Pretty nice, actually.

A: That's good. Let me help you with your things.

B: That's OK. I'm fine.

🎧 **Rhythm and intonation practice**

A **GRAMMAR.** **The past tense of be**

Statements

The weather **was** great.

The fruits and vegetables **were** delicious.

There **was** a terrific restaurant in the hotel.

There **weren't** any problems on the flight.

I He She It	was	We You They	were	**Contractions**
				wasn't = was not
				weren't = were not

Yes / no questions

Was your flight on time?

Were there any good restaurants?

Short answers

Yes, it was. / No, it wasn't.

Yes, there were. / No, there weren't.

Information questions

How was the cruise?

How long was your trip?

How many hours was the flight?

GRAMMAR BOOSTER

PAGES G15–G16
For more . . .

B **Complete the conversations with the past tense of be.**

1. **A:** Did you just get in?

   B: Yes. My flight _____ a little late.

   A: Well, how _____ your vacation?

   B: It was really incredible.

2. **A:** Welcome back! How _____ the drive?

   B: OK. But there _____ a lot of traffic.

   A: Too bad. _____ you alone?

   B: No. My brother _____ with me.

3. A: Where _____ you last week?

B: Me? I _____ at my parents' beach house.

A: Oh. How long _____ you there?

B: About three days.

4. A: So, how _____ your parents' trip?

B: It _____ terrible. They _____ so angry.

A: _____ their train on time?

B: No, it _____. It _____ very late.

 C **VOCABULARY.** Adjectives for travel conditions. Listen and practice.

It was pretty **comfortable**.

It was pretty **scenic**.

It was pretty **boring**.

It was pretty **bumpy**.

It was pretty **scary**.

It was pretty **short / long**.

CONVERSATION PAIR WORK

Practice greeting someone arriving from a flight, drive, cruise, train or bus trip. Use the guide, or create a new conversation.

A: So, how was the _____?
B: Pretty _____, actually.
A: That's _____! Let me help you with your things.
B: _____.

comfortable
scenic } That's good!
short

boring
bumpy } That's too bad!
scary
long

2 Talk about How You Spent Your Free Time

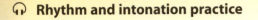

CONVERSATION MODEL Read and listen.

A: What did you do last weekend?
B: Nothing special. What about you?
A: Well, I went to the beach.
B: How was that?
A: I had a really nice time.

🎧 **Rhythm and intonation practice**

A ▸ GRAMMAR. The simple past tense

I		I	
You		You	
He		He	
She	**studied**.	She	**didn't play** tennis.
We		We	
They		They	

Did you **have** a good time?   Yes, I did. / No, I didn't.
Where **did** you **go**?   I went to the beach.
When **did** they **arrive**?   On Tuesday.
What **did** he **do** every day?   He slept until noon.

🎧 **Regular verbs**

| visit | **visited** | play | **played** |
| watch | **watched** | study | **studied** |

Irregular verbs*

buy	**bought**	have	**had**
drink	**drank**	leave	**left**
eat	**ate**	meet	**met**
fly	**flew**	sleep	**slept**
get	**got**	spend	**spent**
go	**went**	take	**took**

*See a complete list on page 128.

GRAMMAR BOOSTER

PAGES G16–G17
For more . . .

B ▸ Complete the sentences with the simple past tense.

Dear Vicky,

We're here! The flight was fine. I _____ the
                                    1. sleep
whole time. Yesterday, we _____ swimming. We
                              2. go
_____ fresh seafood and _____ coconut
  3. eat   4. drink
milk from coconuts right off the trees. In the evening
we _____ a wonderful dinner. After the meal,
      5. have
a jazz ensemble _____ for several hours and
                    6. play
we _____ some very nice people. We _____
      7. meet   8. leave (not)
until after midnight. We _____ such a good
                            9. have
time! This morning we _____ into town and
                          10. walk
_____ postcards. More later! Carol
  11. buy

Vicky Bower

22 High Street

Belleville, NY 10514

USA

LUFTPOST
PAR AVION VIA AEREA

C Complete each question with the simple past tense.

1. **A:** _Where did_ you ___go___ last weekend?   **B:** We went to the beach.
2. **A:** _____ you _____ a good flight?   **B:** Not really. It was pretty scary.
3. **A:** _____ you _____ in the evening?   **B:** We listened to music.
4. **A:** _____ you _____ at the hotel?   **B:** We arrived last Monday.
5. **A:** _____ you _____ lots of souvenirs?   **B:** Yes. We bought some beautiful maps.

D 🎧 **PRONUNCIATION.** **The simple past tense.** **There are three different pronunciations of the simple past tense ending -ed. Read and listen. Then repeat.**

/d/	/t/	/ɪd/
play**ed**	watch**ed**	visit**ed**
rain**ed**	cook**ed**	need**ed**
call**ed**	stopp**ed**	wait**ed**

CONVERSATION PAIR WORK

Talk about how you spent your free time. Use the past time expressions.

A: What did you do _____?
B: _____ . . .

Continue the conversation, using real information or the pictures.

Past time expressions
last weekend
last week
last night
yesterday
over the summer
on your vacation

the zoo

a baseball game

a movie

a museum

3 Discuss Vacation Preferences

A 🎧 **VOCABULARY.** **Adjectives to describe a vacation.** **Listen and practice.**

It was so **relaxing**.

It was so **exciting**.

It was so **interesting**.

It was so **unusual**.

B **READING WARM-UP.** Describe your dream vacation.

C 🎧 **READING.** Read the vacation ads. Then use one or more adjectives from the vocabulary for each vacation.

Exicus

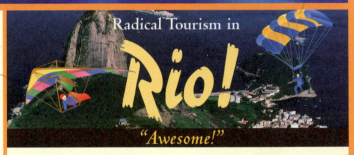

TOP NOTCH TRAVEL *has your dream vacation!*

Bhutan
Secret of the Himalayas

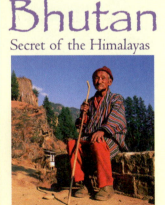

"Everyone was happy to practice their English and walk with us."
Golden

There are many beautiful places on this earth, but Bhutan is unique. Few tourists go there, but you can be one of them. View scenic mountains and meet friendly people dressed in traditional clothing.
www.countrywalkers.com

Radical Tourism in
Rio!

"Awesome!"

Are you looking for EXTREME ADVENTURE? How about skydiving or hang gliding over Rio? Jump with us from a plane flying at over 4,000 meters. Or fly slowly like a bird over the famous white sand beaches and mountains of Rio. As close as it gets to heaven— you won't want to come down! No experience required!
www.rioadventuretours.com

EUROPEAN LANGUAGE TOUR

Enjoy Europe,
Learn a Language!

"I had a great time and I learned so much!"

Attend classes three to four hours a day and have the afternoon free for sightseeing. Stay with a local family—and practice your new language. Study French, Italian, Greek, and more! Classes available for all levels.
www.europeforvisitors.com

sea mountain
inn and spa

"What an experience!"

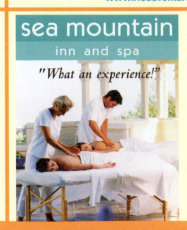

The best of Southern California! Enjoy our scenic Pacific Ocean views. Walk through our Asian gardens and swim in our beautiful pool. Work out in our gym with weights, running machines, or stationary bikes. Eat our delicious and healthful meals and relax with a soothing massage.
www.seamountain.com

D ▸ **PAIR WORK.** Choose a vacation for each person. Use the ads on page 94. Discuss your answers.

❝ I work hard all year. I need a vacation where someone will take care of me. ❞

❝ I love to meet people and learn about new cultures. I'm over fifty, but I like to learn new things. ❞

❝ I'm an athlete and I love sports. I always like to do something new and different. ❞

❝ I like to go to places where other people don't go—'off the beaten path.' ❞

E ▸ **WHAT ABOUT YOU?** Choose a vacation for yourself.

TOP NOTCH INTERACTION

Do You Need a Vacation?

STEP 1. Take the vacation survey. Then compare your answers with a partner.

What's important to you in a vacation? Check ☑ all that apply.

I like
- ❑ exciting vacations
- ❑ relaxing vacations
- ❑ interesting vacations
- ❑ unusual vacations
- ❑ inexpensive vacations
- ❑ _____ vacations

I like vacations with
- ❑ lots of history and culture
- ❑ lots of nature and wildlife
- ❑ lots of sports or physical activities
- ❑ lots of family activities
- ❑ lots of entertainment
- ❑ people who speak my language
- ❑ beautiful hotels
- ❑ great food
- ❑ warm weather
- ❑ nice beaches
- ❑ friendly people
- ❑ _____

STEP 2. GROUP WORK. Discuss vacation preferences with your classmates. Use your survey for support.

- What's important to you in a vacation?
- How often do you go on vacation?
- Do you need a vacation right now? Why?

FREE PRACTICE

4 Tell about Your Experiences on a Trip

LESSON

A ⌒ **VOCABULARY.** **Problems during a trip.** **Listen and practice.**

The weather **was terrible**.

The people **were unfriendly**.

They canceled my flight.

Someone stole my wallet.

B ⌒ **LISTENING COMPREHENSION.** **Listen to the conversations about vacations and check ☑ all the statements that are true.** **Then listen again and check your work.**

1. ☐ Someone stole her car.   ☐ Someone stole her wallet.   ☐ They canceled her flight.
2. ☐ They canceled her flight.   ☐ They canceled her reservation.   ☐ The people were unfriendly.
3. ☐ They canceled her flight.   ☐ The people were unfriendly.   ☐ Her vacation was too short.

C Look at the pictures. Write about the problems.

1. The food _was terrible_ .

2. The waiters _____ .

3. _____ my hotel reservation.

4. _____ my purse.

5. The entertainment _____ .

6. _____ my luggage.

INTERACTION • *How Was Your Vacation?*

STEP 1. **Read two articles students wrote about their vacations.**

> In 2002, I went on vacation to Hawaii. It was very relaxing and the weather was perfect. On the other hand there were some problems. Our hotel wasn't very good. Also, the food was terrible and the waiters and waitresses were unfriendly.

> Last summer, I visited my brother for a week. I took a train and the trip was very scenic. That week, we did a lot of exciting things together. We went horseback riding in the mountains, and we went swimming in the ocean. I also learned how to play golf.

STEP 2. **On the notepad, write notes about a vacation you took.**

place: _____ transportation: _____

weather: _____ food / service / hotel / people: _____

activities: _____

STEP 3. **PAIR WORK.** **Ask about your partner's vacation. Then tell the class about your partner's vacation.**

NEED HELP? **Here's language you already know:**

Ask

How was [the weather]?
What did you do in [the evening]?
Tell me something about ____.
What was wrong with [the food]?
That's [great].
I'm sorry to hear that.
What do you mean?
I'd love to go to ____.

Describe

What do you want to know?
We had a ____ time.
We usually ____.
Sometimes we ____.
The [flight] was [long].
The [beach] was [relaxing].
The [people] were [friendly].

Complain

[The bus driver] drove me crazy!
The ____ didn't work.
The ____ was clogged.
I was in the mood for ____, but …
They didn't accept ____.
The dress code was ____.

STEP 4. **WRITING.** **Write about your vacation. Use your notepad for support.**

A 🎧 **LISTENING COMPREHENSION.** Listen critically to people talking about their travel experiences. Then listen again to complete the sentences. Circle the letter of the best answer.

1. It was very _____. **a.** short **(b.)** scary **c.** scenic
2. It was very _____. **a.** scary **b.** unusual **(c.)** relaxing
3. It was very _____. **(a.)** short **b.** scary **c.** scenic
4. It was very _____. **a.** short **(b.)** scenic **c.** boring

B Complete each sentence or question. Use the past tense form.

1. I _bougt_ a lot of souvenirs on my vacation.
   (buy)
2. Where _____ you _ate_ dinner every night?
   (eat)
3. We _slept_ right on the beach. It _were_ (was) so relaxing.
   (sleep) (be)
4. My sister _got_ back last weekend. She _had_ a great time.
   (get) (have)
5. My friend _ate_ a lot of good food on her trip to Hong Kong.
   (eat)
6. When _____ she _____ at the hotel?
   (arrive)
7. I had a terrible time. The people _were_ very unfriendly.
   (be)
8. We _saw_ an excellent play in London. And it _was_ very inexpensive.
   (see) (be)
9. My wife and I _wert_ running every morning on the beach.
   (go)
10. My brother says he _met_ a lot of friendly people on his trip.
    (meet)

C Complete each conversation with a question in the simple past tense.

1. **A:** _____ on vacation?
   B: We went to Spain.

2. **A:** _____ every evening?
   B: We watched TV and read books.

3. **A:** _____ get back home?
   B: Last night.

🎧 **TOP NOTCH SONG**
"My Dream Vacation"
Lyrics on last book page.

TOP NOTCH PROJECT
Bring in travel ads. In a small group, choose a vacation. Tell the class about it.

TOP NOTCH WEBSITE
For Unit 8 online activities, visit the
Top Notch Companion Website at
www.longman.com/topnotch.

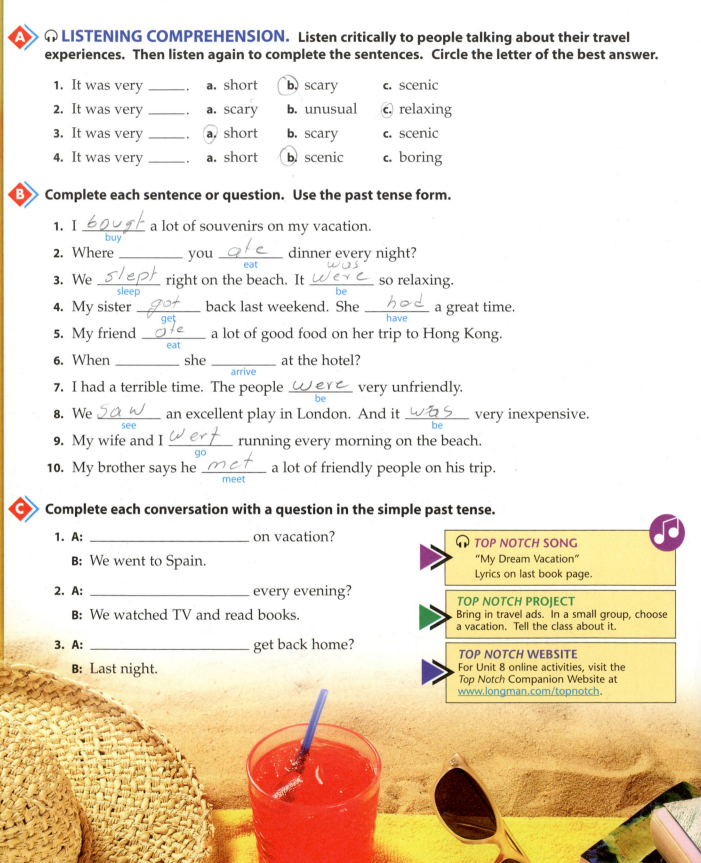

UNIT WRAP-UP

- **Social language.** Create conversations for the people.
  How was your vacation?

- **Grammar.** Talk about the woman's vacation. Use the past tense.

- **Writing.** Write a story about her vacation.
  The flight was very bumpy . . .

Now I can . . .

- ☐ greet someone arriving from a trip.
- ☐ talk about how I spent my free time.
- ☐ discuss vacation preferences.
- ☐ tell about my experiences on a trip.

Taking Transportation

UNIT GOALS

1 Discuss schedules and buy tickets
2 Book travel services
3 Understand airport announcements
4 Describe transportation problems

A **TOPIC PREVIEW.** Look carefully at the departure schedule and the clock. What time is the next flight to São Paulo?

RAPID AIR BRASILIA DEPARTURES

Destination	FLT/No.	Departs	Gate	Status
São Paulo	56	15:50	G4	departed
Belo Horizonte	267	16:10	G3	boarding
Rio de Janeiro	89	16:10	G9	boarding
São Paulo	58	16:50	G4	now 17:25
São Luis	902	17:00	G3	on time
São Paulo	60	17:50	G4	delayed
Porto Alegre	763	17:50	G3	on time
Caracas	04	18:05	G1	canceled
Rio de Janeiro	91	18:10	G9	on time
São Paulo	62	18:50	G4	on time

15:50

"My mom went to Cheju in 2002. She took Asiana."

B **DISCUSSION.** How often do you fly? Complete the chart with flights you took or that someone you know took. Tell your class about them.

Destination	Year	Airline
Cheju, Korea	2002	Asiana

C 🎧 **SOUND BITES.** **Read along silently as you listen to a natural conversation.**

MARMO: Excuse me. Do you speak English?

ROBERT: Yes. But actually I'm French.

MARMO: I'm looking for the bullet train.

ROBERT: Which one?

MARMO: The Nozomi. To Kyoto. Leaving at 10:20.

ROBERT: I'm taking that, too. You can follow me. It leaves from track 15.

MARMO: Thanks. But we should hurry. It's going to leave in seven minutes.

ROBERT: By the way, where are you from?

MARMO: Jakarta. I'm Indonesian.

ROBERT: No kidding! I'm going to Indonesia next week.

MARMO: Really? What a small world!

D **Read the statements critically. Check ☑ the statements that you are sure are true.**

☐ **1.** The Nozomi is a bullet train.
☑ **2.** Both travelers are taking the bullet train.
☑ **3.** The train is going to leave soon.
☐ **4.** Robert goes to Indonesia often.

WHAT ABOUT **YOU?**

What are your travel plans?

🌐 TRAVEL SURVEY

Where are you going to travel in the next few years?
☐ Asia ☑ Africa ☐ Europe
☐ North America ☐ South America ☐ Other _____

What means of transportation are you going to take?
☑ Airplane ☐ Ship ☐ Car
☐ Train ☐ Bus ☐ Other _____

What language(s) are you going to speak on your trip?
☐ My native language ☑ English ☐ Other _____

Discuss Schedules and Buy Tickets

CONVERSATION MODEL Read and listen..

A: Can we make the 2:00 bus to Puebla?

B: No, I'm sorry. It left five minutes ago.

A: Oh, no! What should we do?

B: Well, you could take the 2:30.

A: OK. Two tickets, please.

B: One way or round trip?

A: Round trip.

Rhythm and intonation practice

A **VOCABULARY.** **Tickets and trips.** **Listen and practice.**

PASSENGER TICKET
KOREA BUS LINE
SEOUL > SOKCHO

a one-way ticket

PASSENGER TICKET
KOREA BUS LINE
SEOUL > SOKCHO
SOKCHO > SEOUL

a round-trip ticket

JAPAN RAIL	Kodama (local)	Nozomi (express)
Tokyo	10:13	10:20
Odawara	10:30	–
Atami	11:00	–
Maibara	13:39	–
Kyoto	14:04	12:38

a local   an express

Air China
Flight
009
New York → Los Angeles → Taipei

a direct flight

Air China
Flight
808
New York ⟶ Taipei

a non-stop flight

an aisle seat   a window seat

B **Complete the conversations with appropriate words and phrases from the vocabulary.**

1. A: Would you like a window or an aisle?

B: _____. I need to stretch my legs.

2. A: Is Flight 009 a _____ flight?

B: No. It's a _____ flight. It makes two stops, but you don't have to change planes.

3. A: Do you want a _____ ticket?

B: Actually, I need a one-way ticket.

4. A: I'm sorry. You missed the express.

B: Oh, no! Well, can I still make the _____?

5. A: Do you want the window or the aisle?

B: I'd like the _____, please. I hear the mountains are beautiful.

C ▸ GRAMMAR. could and should

could *cuanto hay posibildade*

Use **could** and the base form of a verb to suggest an alternative or a possibility.

The express bus is full. You **could take** the local instead.

---

should *conseo*

Use **should** and the base form of a verb to give advice.

You **shouldn't take** that flight. You **should take** the non-stop.

Questions

Could I **take** the 2:20?	Yes, you **could**. / No, you **couldn't**.
Who **should get** the aisle seat?	I **should**. I like to walk around.

GRAMMAR BOOSTER

PAGES G17–G18
For more . . .

D ▸ Complete each sentence or question with **should** or **could** and the base form of the verb.

1. When *should we leave* for the airport? There's going to be a lot of traffic.

(we / leave)

2. *they shouldn't take* the local bus. It makes too many stops.

(They / not take)

3. You have two options. *You could take* the express bus or *you could fly*.

(You / take) ... (you / fly)

4. That train's always crowded. *He should get* his ticket in advance.

(He / get)

5. *He could buy* it at a travel agency, but it's cheaper on the Internet.

(He / buy)

6. Tell her *she should choose* the direct flight. It's better than changing planes.

(she / choose)

CONVERSATION PAIR WORK

Discuss schedules and tickets. Use the train departure board and the clock. Use the guide, or create a new conversation.

A: Can I make the _____ to _____?
B: No, I'm sorry. It left _____ ago.
A: _____! What should I do?
B: Well, you could take the _____.
A: _____ …

Continue the conversation any way you like.

DEPARTURES   7:26 A.M.

To	Departs	Track
WASHINGTON	7:10	6
BOSTON	7:22	9
PHILADELPHIA	7:25	19
WASHINGTON	8:25	8
BOSTON	8:26	24
PHILADELPHIA	8:31	18

CONTROLLED PRACTICE

Book Travel Services

⌒ CONVERSATION MODEL Read and listen.

A: I'm going to need a rental car in Dubai.
B: Certainly. What date are you arriving?
A: April 6th.
B: What time do you get in?
A: Let me check . . . 5:45.

⌒ **Rhythm and intonation practice**

A ⌒ **VOCABULARY. Travel services. Listen and practice.**

a rental car a taxi a limousine a hotel reservation

B ⌒ **LISTENING COMPREHENSION. Listen to the conversations about travel services. Then listen again and write the service each client needs. Listen again if necessary to check your work.**

1. _a limousine_
2. _a hotel reservation_
3. _a rental car_
4. _a taxi_

C GRAMMAR. Be going to for the future

Use <u>be going to</u> + the base form of a verb to talk about the future.

<u>be</u>	<u>going to</u>	**base form**
I'm	going to	**rent** a car in New York.
She's	going to	**be** at the airport.
We're	going to	**take** a taxi into town.

Are they going to get a round-trip ticket?   Yes, they are. / No, they aren't.
Who's going to make the reservation?   We are.
When are you going to call?   At 8:00.

Remember: The present continuous and the simple present tense can also express future actions.
We're **flying** to Madrid. The plane **leaves** at 6:00.

GRAMMAR BOOSTER

**PAGES G18–G19
For more . . .**

D Complete each sentence or question with <u>be going to</u> and the base form of the verb.

1. _they are going to buy_ tickets for the express.
   they / buy

2. When _is she going to call_ the travel agent?
   she / call

3. _are we going to reserve_ seats for everyone or just for us?
   we / reserve

4. Who _is going to meet_ him at the airport?
   meet

E Complete the e-mail. Circle the correct forms.

Here's my travel information: I (**1.** leaving / **'m leaving**) Mexico City at 4:45 P.M. on Atlas Airlines flight 6702. The flight (**2.** arriving / **arrives**) in Chicago at 9:50 P.M. Mara's flight (**3.** be going to get in / **is getting in**) ten minutes later, so we (**4.** **'re meeting** / meeting) at the baggage claim. That's too late for you to pick me up, so I (**5.** **'m going to take** / taking) a limo from O'Hare. Mara (**6.** goes to / **is going to**) come along and (**7.** **spend** / spending) the night with us. Her flight to Tokyo (**8.** not leaving / **doesn't leave**) until the next day.

CONVERSATION
PAIR WORK

Book a rental car, taxi, limousine, or hotel. Use the tickets for arrival information. Use the guide, or create a new conversation.

PASSENGER TICKET AND BAGGAGE CHECK
AIR CUZCO APRIL 11 FLIGHT 22
DEPARTURE: 18:00 ARRIVAL: 19:15
LIMA TO CUZCO
88985376124 0 988 7631986534 7

BOARDING PASS
EXCELA RAIL TRANSPORT
JUNE 26 EXPRESS TRAIN
NEW YORK TO WASHINGTON
DEPARTURE: 6:00PM
ARRIVAL: 9:10 PM

Seoul Touristbus
FROM Seoul
TO Sokcho
DATE 13 August
DEPARTS 07:45
ARRIVES 11:55

A: I'm going to need _rental car_ in _Lima._

B: _Certainly._ What date are you arriving?

A: _April 11_

B: What time does the _flight_ arrive?

A: Let me check.... _19 15_.

B: _Real._

Continue the conversation in your <u>own</u> way . . .

Ideas
Are you going to need a hotel reservation, too?
How long are you going to stay?

CONTROLLED PRACTICE

3 Understand Airport Announcements

A 🎧 **VOCABULARY.** Airline passenger information. **Listen and practice.**

a passenger | an agent
a boarding pass

security

an overbooking

a cancellation

B 🎧 **LISTENING COMPREHENSION.** Listen to the airport announcements and check ☑ the problems that are announced.

☐ a delay   ☑ a gate change
☐ a cancellation   ☐ a security problem
☐ an overbooking   ☑ a mechanical problem

C 🎧 **Now listen again and write the flight information.**

1. flight number: _692_
2. original departure gate: _26B_

3. final departure gate: _16C_
4. final departure time: _7 pm_

D 🎧 **PRONUNCIATION.** Stating alternatives. **Listen to the rhythm and intonation of alternatives. Then listen again and repeat.**

- Well, you could take the train, or take the bus.

- They could wait or reserve a later flight.

- Would you like a one-way ticket or a round-trip ticket?

Antofagasta, Chile

INTERACTION • *Overbooked!*

STEP 1. Read the announcement by the gate agent for Rapid Air flight 58 from Brasilia to São Paulo.

Good afternoon, ladies and gentlemen. Flight 58 is overbooked. We apologize. We need one volunteer to give up a seat on this flight.

There are seats available on all later flights to São Paulo. If you volunteer to take a later flight, Rapid Air will give you a free round-trip ticket anywhere. The free ticket is good for one year.

16:35

RAPIDAIR
GATE G9

DESTINATION	FLIGHT	DEPARTS	STATUS
São Paulo	58	Now 17:25	See Agent

STEP 2. PAIR WORK. You and your partner have tickets on Flight 58. Read the facts.

- The time is now 16:35.
- You have a very important dinner in São Paulo at 20:30.
- The flight takes two hours.

Now look at the departure schedule and discuss your alternatives.

DEPARTURES			
São Paulo	56	16:20	departed
Rio de Janeiro	89	16:40	boarding
São Paulo	58	16:50	now 17:25
São Paulo	60	17:50	on time

What are you going to do?

I'm going to volunteer.

NEED HELP? Here's language you already know:

Discuss plans

What are you going to do?	It departed ____ ago.
What should we do?	What time does ____ arrive?
You could ____.	
We should ____.	Is it direct / non-stop?
What about ____?	I'm going to ____.
Can we make the ____?	

STEP 3. DISCUSSION. Tell the class what you decided and why. How many students decided to take a later flight?

Boomas

4 Describe Transportation Problems

A 🎧 **VOCABULARY.** **Transportation problems.** **Listen and practice.**

We **had an accident**.

We **had mechanical problems**.

We **missed our train**.

We **got bumped** from the flight.

We **got seasick**.

B 🎧 **LISTENING COMPREHENSION.** **Listen to the conversations. Then listen again and complete each statement with a phrase from the vocabulary.**

1. They got _scosik_.
2. They had _accident_.
3. They got _bumped_ _t.._.
4. They had _mehaniced_ _m.._.
5. They missed _flight_.

C **READING WARM-UP.** **Do your trips always go well?**

D 🎧 **READING.** **Read the news clippings. Which clipping is the most interesting? Explain your opinion.**

Runaway train travels 70 miles

A train from the CSX Company left Stanley Yard today when the engineer accidentally hit the power lever instead of the brake. The train was caught 70 miles later, near Toledo, Ohio. There were no injuries.

MYSTERY CRUISE SHIP ILLNESSES END

Incidents of sickness are now over, according to a cruise industry spokesperson. He was referring to numerous outbreaks of illness on cruises in recent weeks.

Dave Forney of the Centers for Disease Control and Prevention agrees. Poor sanitation in handling food was probably responsible for the recent outbreaks. "It's always important to wash hands and prepare food safely," adds Forney.

TURKEYS ENTER COCKPIT

On March 9, a small plane operated by Atlantic Coast Airlines was en route from Dulles International Airport near Washington to LaGuardia Airport in New York, when the aircraft was struck by two wild turkeys. There were four crew members and fifty passengers on board. The pilot reported that the turkeys entered the cockpit through the pilot's window. No one was injured.

SOURCES: cnn.com and ntsb.gov

E **Complete each statement to predict what each person probably said.**

1. The train engineer probably said, "_____."
   a. I almost had an accident.
   b. I almost missed the train.

2. The cruise industry spokesperson probably said, "_____."
   a. The passengers ate bad food.
   b. The passengers got seasick.

3. The pilot of the plane probably said, "_____."
   a. We had mechanical problems.
   b. We almost had an accident.

TOP NOTCH **INTERACTION** • *Travel Woes*

STEP 1. **Circle all the transportation you have taken. Then add other transportation you have taken.**

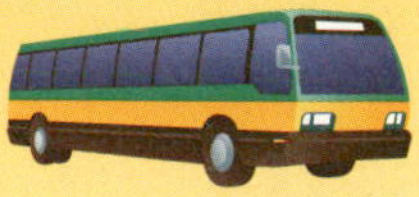

bus

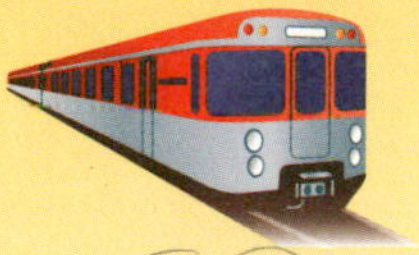

train

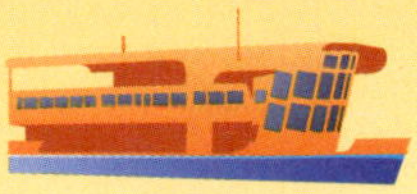

ferry

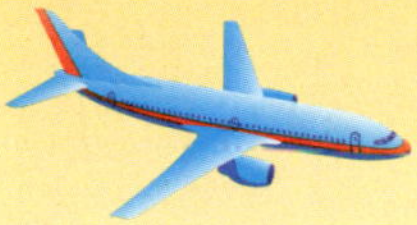

airplane

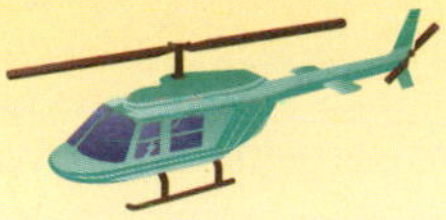

helicopter

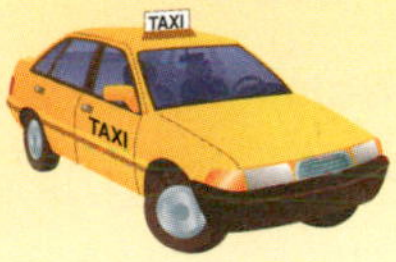

taxi

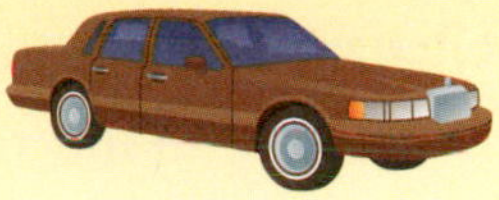

limousine

other ______

STEP 2. **Ask your partner questions about the transportation he or she circled.**

> "When was the last time you took a train?"

STEP 3. **Choose a trip when you had transportation problems. On the notepad, make notes about the trip.**

means of transportation: ______

when: ______

destination: ______

good memories: ______

problems: ______

STEP 4. **GROUP WORK.** **Tell your story to the class. Ask your classmates questions about their trips.**

STEP 5. **WRITING.** **Write the true story of what happened. Use your notepad for support.**

Last summer I went to Tanzania. I traveled from Dar es Salaam to Songea. The bus was very comfortable and not expensive. It had air-conditioning and a bathroom. But I always get bus sick, so …

FREE PRACTICE

UNIT 9
CHECKPOINT

A 🎧 **LISTENING COMPREHENSION.** Listen to the conversations. Then listen again and write the number of the conversation below each picture.

_5_   _3_   _1_   _4_   _2_

B Complete each sentence with an appropriate word or phrase.

1. If you don't want to drive to the airport, a ___taxi___ is very convenient and practical.

2. A ___limousin___ is a large car with a driver.

3. If you are not returning, you should buy a ___one way___ ticket.

4. A ___Non stop___ flight is faster than a direct flight.

5. In order to board a plane, you have to give a ___boarding pass___ to the agent at the gate.

C Write an answer to each statement.

1. "Can we still make the 6:00 ferry?" **YOU** _Yes, we can. – No, we can't_.

2. "Why are you buying a one-way ticket?" **YOU** _Because I am not return_.

3. "Oh, no! When did it leave?" **YOU** _It left ten minis ago_.

D Complete the conversation with **be going to** and the indicated verbs.

A: On Saturday, _we are going_ for Cancun.
   1. we / leave

B: Really? _Are you renting_ a car there? There are some great
   2. you / rent

   places to explore.

A: No. I think _we are_ on the beach and rest.
   3. we / stay

   By the way, where _are_ for your vacation?
   4. you and Margo / go

B: I'm not sure. But _I'm going_ to Bangkok on business
   5. I / travel

   next month. And _In_ a few days off to go
   6. I / take

   sightseeing. I hear it's great.

E **WRITING.** On a separate sheet of paper, write a paragraph about your next trip. Use the questions for support.

- Where are you going to go?
- What kind of transportation are you going to take?
- When do you leave?
- Who are you traveling with?
- What are you going to do when you are there?
- When do you get back?

TOP NOTCH PROJECT
Use the Internet to plan travel arrangements. Use real schedules and travel services.

TOP NOTCH WEBSITE
For Unit 9 online activities, visit the *Top Notch* Companion Website at www.longman.com/topnotch.

- **Social language.** Choose one picture. Create a conversation for the people. Use <u>could</u> and <u>should</u>.
- **Writing.** Tell the story in the pictures. Use the times and dates.

> ✔ **Now I can . . .**
> - ☐ discuss schedules and buy tickets.
> - ☐ book travel services.
> - ☐ understand airport announcements.
> - ☐ describe transportation problems.

Shopping Smart

UNIT GOALS

1 Ask for a recommendation
2 Bargain for a lower price
3 Discuss tipping customs
4 Talk about a shopping experience

A ▷ **TOPIC PREVIEW.** Look at the information in the travel guide for Toronto. Do you ever use traveler's checks, credit cards, or ATMs?

When you're in TORONTO ...

TRAVELER'S CHECKS ▶
The easiest and safest way to carry money in Canada is in traveler's checks.

◀ CHANGING MONEY
Banks usually offer the best exchange rates. Remember to bring your passport.

▼ CREDIT CARDS
You can use credit cards at most stores and restaurants. However, some smaller businesses don't accept them. Make sure you always carry some cash.

ATMs ▶
Get cash 24 hours a day from ATMs (called *bank machines* in Canada) at banks, bus and train stations, and large supermarkets.

▲ TIPPING
Leave a tip of about 10–15% of a restaurant bill or taxi fare. Restaurant bills for larger groups may include a service charge. Also tip hairdressers and hotel staff.

BARGAINING ▶
While shopping in Toronto, it's generally not the custom to bargain for a lower price.

75!
50!
65!

SOURCE: based on information from www.roughguides.com

B ▷ **DISCUSSION.** How do you pay for things when you travel? Do you usually bargain for a lower price when you go shopping? Where is it OK to bargain? Are you a good bargainer?

C 🎧 **SOUND BITES.** **Read along silently as you listen to a natural conversation.**

KAY: Oh, no. I'm almost out of cash. And I'm looking for a gift for my mother.

AMY: That's OK. I'm sure these shops accept credit cards. Let's go in here. They have really nice stuff.

KAY: Good idea.

AMY: What about this?

KAY: It's gorgeous, but it's a bit more than I want to spend.

AMY: Maybe you could get a better price.

KAY: You think so?

AMY: Well, it can't hurt to ask.

D **UNDERSTANDING MEANING FROM CONTEXT.** **Choose the best answer.**

1. When Kay says, "I'm almost out of cash," she means _____.
   a. I don't have much money.   b. I have a lot of money.

2. When Amy says, "It can't hurt to ask," she means _____.
   a. It's a good idea to ask.   b. It's not a good idea to ask.

3. When Kay says, "It's gorgeous," she means _____.
   a. It's very pretty.   b. I don't really like it.

4. When Amy says, "Maybe you could get a better price," she means _____.
   a. This is a good price.   b. Bargain with the salesperson.

WHAT ABOUT **YOU?**

What do _you_ usually do when you're out of cash?

- ☐ I go to the bank.
- ☐ I use a credit card.
- ☐ I get money from an ATM.
- ☐ other _____.

1 ▶ **Ask for a Recommendation**

🎧 **CONVERSATION MODEL** Read and listen.

A: I'm looking for a digital camera. Which is the least expensive?

B: The X80. But it's not the best. How much can you spend?

A: No more than 350.

B: Well, we've got some good ones in your price range.

A: Great. Could I have a look?

🎧 **Rhythm and intonation practice**

A ▶ **GRAMMAR. Superlative adjectives**

Use superlative adjectives to compare more than two people, places, or things.

Which camera is **the cheapest** of these three?
Which brands are **the most popular** in your store?

adjective	comparative	superlative	adjective	comparative	superlative
cheap	cheaper	**the cheapest**	comfortable	more comfortable	**the most comfortable**
nice	nicer	**the nicest**	portable	more portable	**the most portable**
easy	easier	**the easiest**	difficult	less difficult	**the least difficult**
big	bigger	**the biggest**	expensive	less expensive	**the least expensive**

> **Irregular forms**
> good → better → **the best**
> bad → worse → **the worst**

GRAMMAR BOOSTER

PAGES G19–G20
For more …

B ▶ **Write the superlative form of the adjective. Use the.**

1. **A:** All of these cameras are easy to use.

   B: But which is _____?
   small

2. **A:** All of our sweaters are pretty warm.

   B: But which brand makes _____ ones?
   heavy

3. **A:** She wrote at least six books about Italy. They're pretty interesting.

   B: Which of her books is _____?
   interesting

4. **A:** Do you want to take a taxi, bus, or train to the airport?

   B: Which is _____?
   convenient

C 🎧 **VOCABULARY.** Electronic products. Listen and practice.

a digital camera

a camcorder

a DVD player

an MP3 player

a scanner

D 🎧 **LISTENING COMPREHENSION.** Listen to the conversations at an electronics store. Then listen again and write the electronic product the people are talking about.

1. _____ 2. _____ 3. _____ 4. _____

CONVERSATION
PAIR WORK

Ask for a recommendation. Use the ads, changing the prices to local currency if you wish. You can use this guide, or create a new conversation.

A: I'm looking for _____.
Which is the _____?

B: The _____. But it's not _____.
How much can you spend?

A: No more than _____.

B: _____ …

Continue the conversation in your <u>own</u> way . . .

Ideas
the nicest
the most popular
the lightest
the most practical
the easiest to use

MP3 Players

RICO SL-S225 **$129** *Practical*

PUSAN X23 **$109** *Easy to Use*

POWER X MUSIC MASTER **NEW! $199**

Digital Cameras

HONSHU X24 **$209** *Very Popular*

HONSHU B100 **$149**

PREGO 5 **NEW! $299**

Camcorders

VISION 720 **$949** *Very Light*

PUSAN 5X **$829** *Easy to Use*

DIEGO P500 **$679** *Popular*

CONTROLLED PRACTICE

Bargain for a Lower Price

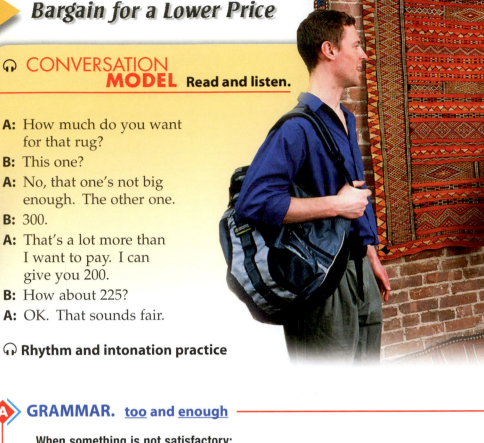

🎧 **CONVERSATION MODEL** **Read and listen.**

A: How much do you want for that rug?

B: This one?

A: No, that one's not big enough. The other one.

B: 300.

A: That's a lot more than I want to pay. I can give you 200.

B: How about 225?

A: OK. That sounds fair.

🎧 **Rhythm and intonation practice**

A ▶ **GRAMMAR.** **too** and **enough**

> **When something is not satisfactory:**
>
> | | | |
> |---|---|---|
> | Those rugs are **too small**. | OR | Those rugs are **not big enough**. |
> | That camera is **too heavy**. | OR | That camera is **not light enough**. |
>
> **When something is satisfactory:**
>
> This PDA is **small enough**. I'll take it.

GRAMMAR BOOSTER

PAGE G21
For more . . .

B ▶ Complete the conversations with the adjectives from the box. Use **too** or **enough**.

> noisy   fast   expensive   small   hot   big

1. A: That microwave oven needs to be _____ for my family. We're very busy.

B: Oh, yes. The X11 is our fastest model.

2. A: These pumps aren't _____. They're very uncomfortable.

B: I'm so sorry. Let me get you a larger size.

3. A: My photocopier is _____. It's driving me crazy!

B: Then let me show you a quieter model.

4. A: We ordered the <u>hot</u> appetizers. These aren't _____.

    B: Of course, sir. I'll take care of that right away.

5. A: How about this pocket TV? It's pretty small.

    B: That's definitely _____. Thanks.

6. A: This jacket is a bargain. It's only $495.

    B: I'm sorry. That's just _____ for me.

C 🎧 **PRONUNCIATION.** **Confirming and clarifying information.** **Listen to the rising intonation to confirm. Then repeat.**

A: How much is that rug?

B: This one?

A: That's right.

A: Could I have a look at that sweater?

B: The red one?

A: No, the black one.

D 🎧 **VOCABULARY.** **Handicrafts.** **Listen and practice.**

a painting

a plate

a rug

a bowl

a vase

a necklace

CONVERSATION
PAIR WORK

With a partner, bargain for a lower price. Use the pictures above, giving a price to each item. Start like this:

A: How much do you want for that _____?
B: This one?
A: _____ …

Continue the conversation in your <u>own</u> way . . .

3 Discuss Tipping Customs

A **READING WARM-UP.** Do you think tipping is a good idea or a bad idea?

B 🎧 **READING.** Read the article about tipping customs. Is any of the information surprising to you? Explain.

Did you remember to leave a tip?

In some countries tipping is very common. In others, tipping is not expected. Here are some tipping customs from around the world.

Australia

Australians are pretty relaxed about tips—people do not usually expect them. Many people will be quite surprised if you give them a tip. Customers do leave a 10–15% tip in nicer restaurants, but don't tip taxi drivers. Instead, you can just say "Keep the change," and round off the fare.

France

A service charge is almost always included on the bill in restaurants and cafés. If you are satisfied with the service, leave an additional small tip for the server. Tip porters about 1 euro for each piece of luggage, and leave the maid who cleans your hotel room about 1 euro per day. Taxi drivers expect 10–15% of the fare. And don't forget to tip your tour guide.

US and Canada

Tip waiters and taxi drivers anywhere from 15–20% of the total bill—depending on how satisfied you are with the service. A service charge is sometimes added to a restaurant bill if there are six or more people at the table, so you don't have to leave an additional tip. At airports and hotels, porters expect about $1 per bag. In some fast-food restaurants and coffee bars, there is a cup for small tips near the cashier.

Note: In some countries, it's not customary to give tips. Before you travel, check local tipping customs to be sure.

SOURCES: *Lonely Planet, Rough Guide, Fodor's* travel guides

C Read each person's question about tipping. Then give each person advice, according to the reading.

❝ I'm going to Paris, France. I'm staying in a small hotel for about six days. How much should I tip the maid? ❞

❝ I'm studying English in Sydney, Australia, and I just took a taxi home. The fare is AUS$3.60. How much should I give the taxi driver? ❞

❝ I'm visiting friends in Los Angeles, in the United States. I took ten people out for dinner. The bill is US$360. How much more should I leave for the tip? ❞

❝ I just arrived in Montreal, Canada, and took a taxi from the airport. The fare is CAN$6.90. How much should I tip the driver? ❞

STEP 1. What are your opinions about tipping when traveling in a country where tipping is customary? Take the opinion poll. Then compare your answers with your class.

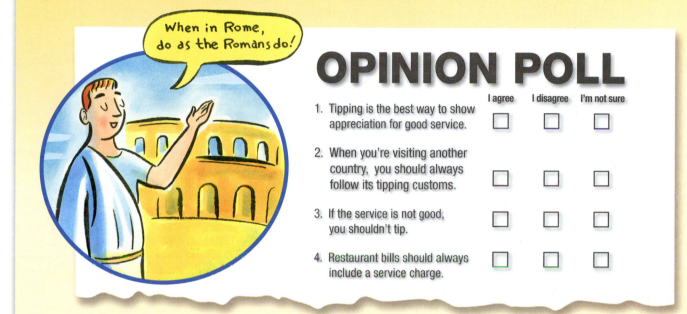

STEP 2. PAIR WORK. On the notepad, write some suggestions for showing appreciation for good service in this country. If tipping is customary, explain how much to tip.

waiters / waitresses:

taxi drivers:

hotel maids:

baggage porters:

other:

STEP 3. GROUP WORK. In small groups, compare your notes. Does everyone agree?

FREE PRACTICE

Talk about a Shopping Experience

LESSON 4

A 🎧 **VOCABULARY.** **Talking about prices.** **Listen and practice.**

She got a good price.

She saved a lot of money.

He paid too much.

NOTE: Prices can be converted to local currency if you wish.

B 🎧 **LISTENING COMPREHENSION.** **Listen to the conversations about shopping. Then listen again and complete the chart.**

What did the shopper buy?	got a good price	saved a lot of money	paid too much
1. _a bowl_	✔	☐	☐
2.	☐	☐	☐
3.	☐	☐	☐
4.	☐	☐	☐

C **DISCUSSION.** **Read this true story about a shopping experience. Then discuss the questions.**

Several years ago, I was in Saudi Arabia on business, and I wanted to buy a small rug. I wanted to spend no more than $350 USD. I found a beautiful and unusual rug, but the asking price was too high for me: $900. The salesman and I talked about the price for a long time. Finally, he shook my hand, and I thought that was the end of the conversation.

I left the store, and he looked very surprised. Then I was surprised! He actually had agreed to my offer of $350. That's why he shook my hand. Of course, I bought the rug. What a great deal!

1. How much money did the salesman want? How much did the shopper pay?

2. Why was the shopper surprised?

3. Do you think the shopper got a good price?

INTERACTION • *It's the Best!*

STEP 1. PAIR WORK. Discuss the questions with a partner.

1. In your own city or town, what is ...
   • the best restaurant?
   • the nicest hotel?
   • the most expensive department store?
   • the most unusual market?
   • the most interesting museum?

2. Where can you buy ...
   • the least expensive fruits and vegetables?
   • the nicest flowers?
   • the best electronics products?
   • the most unusual souvenirs?
   • the wildest clothes?

STEP 2. DISCUSSION. Discuss your choices.

> " The Savoy Hotel has the biggest rooms and the best food. "

> " The Central Market is too expensive. The fruits and vegetables at the Old Town Market are much better and cheaper. "

STEP 3. On your notepad, write notes about a good or bad shopping experience you had. Then tell the class about your experience.

What did you buy?
Where did you buy it?
How much money did the salesperson want?
Did you bargain?
How much did you pay?

STEP 4. WRITING. Write the story of your shopping experience.

UNIT 10
CHECKPOINT

A 🎧 **LISTENING COMPREHENSION.** Listen to the conversations and write the name of the item. Then listen again critically. Check ✓ if the item is satisfactory or not satisfactory to the customer.

		satisfactory	not satisfactory
1.	_a camcorder_	☐	☑
2.	_____	☐	☐
3.	_____	☐	☐
4.	_____	☐	☐

B **Complete the sentences.**

1. If you're out of cash, you can get money from _____.

2. If there's a service charge on the restaurant bill, you don't have to leave a _____.

3. In many countries, it's OK to _____ for a lower price.

4. You can get the best _____ at banks.

5. _____ are a safe and easy way to carry money when traveling.

6. What a ripoff. I paid _____.

7. Wow! What a great deal. I _____ a lot of money.

C **Write each sentence in another way. Use _too_ or _enough_.**

1. That vase is too heavy. _That vase isn't light enough_____.

2. Those cameras aren't cheap enough. _____.

3. This PDA is too big. _____.

4. These drinks aren't cold enough. _____.

5. That restaurant is too noisy. _____.

D **Write sentences about stores in your city. Use the superlative.**

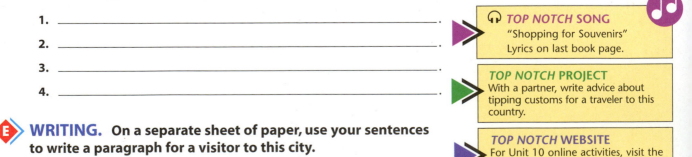

Winston's Department Store has the cheapest clothing.

1. _____.

2. _____.

3. _____.

4. _____.

🎧 *TOP NOTCH* **SONG**
"Shopping for Souvenirs"
Lyrics on last book page.

TOP NOTCH **PROJECT**
With a partner, write advice about tipping customs for a traveler to this country.

TOP NOTCH **WEBSITE**
For Unit 10 online activities, visit the *Top Notch* Companion Website at www.longman.com/topnotch.

E **WRITING.** On a separate sheet of paper, use your sentences to write a paragraph for a visitor to this city.

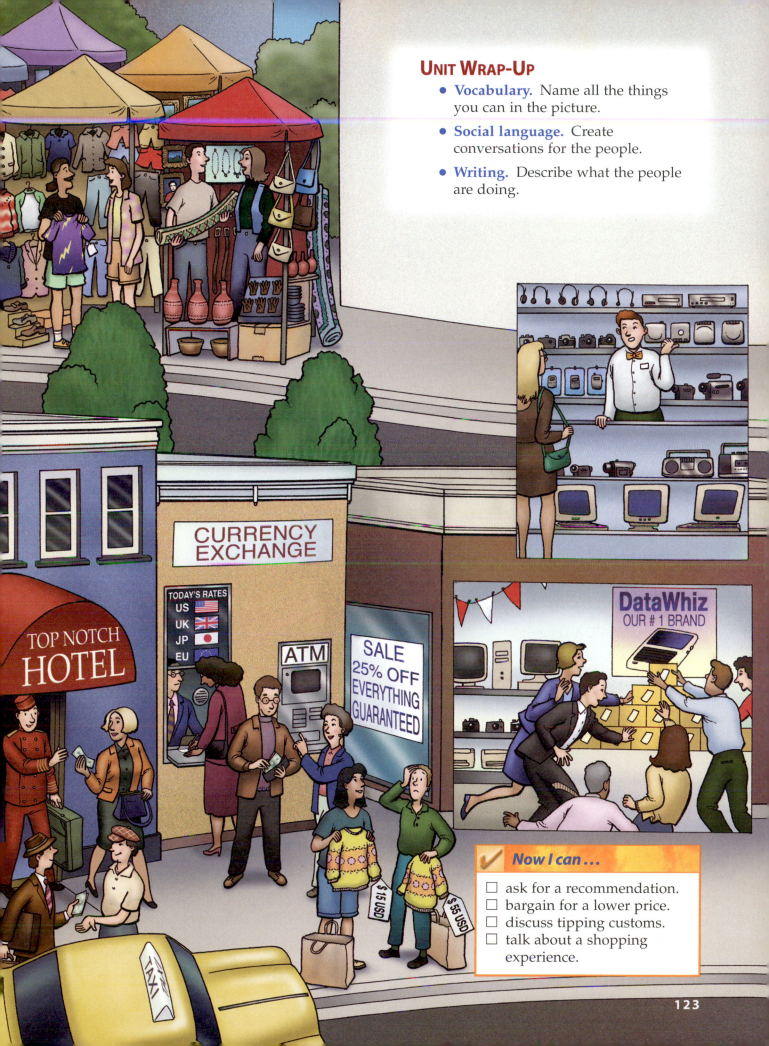

UNIT WRAP-UP

- **Vocabulary.** Name all the things you can in the picture.
- **Social language.** Create conversations for the people.
- **Writing.** Describe what the people are doing.

✔ **Now I can ...**

☐ ask for a recommendation.
☐ bargain for a lower price.
☐ discuss tipping customs.
☐ talk about a shopping experience.

Alphabetical word list

This is an alphabetical list of all productive vocabulary in the *Top Notch 1* units. The numbers refer to the page on which the word first appears or is defined. When a word has two meanings, both are in the list.

A

a/an   56
absolutely   80
accept   58
accessory   76
accident   108
across the street   20
activity   88
actress   5
address   20
aerobics   64
agent   106
air-conditioning   48
airline   105
airplane   109
airport   66
aisle seat   102
alike   34
almost always   68
always   68
amazing   89
an   56
another   79
appetizer   52
apple   55
appliance   45
appropriate   84
around the corner   20
arrival   102
arrive   100
art exhibit   19
artist   6
at   18
athlete   6
athletic field   69
ATM   112
aunt   28
avoid   70
awesome   42
awful   44

B

back   82
bad   78
bag   76
baggage porter   118
banana   55
bank   113
bargain   116
baseball game   93
basement   82
basketball   64

basketball player   5
bathrobe   76
bathroom   45
be   90
beach   89
beautiful   78
bedroom   45
bedtime   17
beef   55
belt   76
better   78
between   20
beverage   52
big   78
bike riding   64
black   79
blazer   80
blond   38
blue   81
boarding pass   105
book   104
boring   91
both   34
bottled water   53
boxers   76
brand   42
bread   55
briefs   79
broccoli   55
brother   28
brother-in-law   28
brown   78
bullet train   101
bumpy   90
bus   109
business   4
busy   18
but   34
butter   55
buy   77

C

cake   55
call   93
camcorder   115
can   66
cancel   96
cancellation   106
candy   55
cardigan   80
carrot   55
cash   80
casual   83
CD burner   43
CD player   44

cell phone   43
certainly   80
change money   112
charge   80
cheap   78
check   58
cheese   55
chef   10
chicken   55
child   28
choice   53
clam   55
class   6
classical music   16
classmates   8
clean   64
clerk   77
clogged   48
close   48
clothes   76
clothing   79
coat   82
coconut oil   55
coffee   54
coffee maker   44
coffee shop   82
color   79
come   8
comfortable   91
complain   48
complaint   48
computer programmer   10
concert   19
conservative   85
convenient   46
cook   64
cookie   55
corn oil   55
corner   20
couch potato   65
could   103
cousin   28
crab   55
crazy   41
credit card   58
crew neck   80
cruise   90
culture   84
cute   29

D

dairy product   55
dancing   64
dark   86

daughter   5
decline   18
delay   106
delayed   100
delicious   57
depart   100
department   76
department store   76
departure   102
dessert   53
destination   109
different   34
difficult   114
digital camera   115
dinner   64
direct flight   102
directions   20
dish   57
divorced   31
do aerobics   64
down the street   20
dress   78
dress code   85
drink   92
DVD player   115

E

early   17
easy   114
eat   54
egg   54
either   34
electronic product   115
electronics   43
elevator   82
e-mail address   11
English   64
enough   116
entertainment   19
entrée   52
escalator   82
evening   68
event   19
every day   65
every weekend   65
exciting   94
expensive   78
express   102

F

fair   116
family   28

family member   31
family name   4
fan   17
fast   116
father   28
father-in-law   28
fatty   60
favorite   24
fax machine   44
ferry   109
fine   78
first   82
first name   4
fish   55
flats   80
flight   90
flight attendant   10
flight number   105
flush   48
fly   92
food   55
free   18
fridge   48
fried   56
from   6
front   82
fruit   55
funny sound   48

G

gadget   40
gate   105
get   92
get bumped   108
get seasick   108
get to know   4
get up   72
gift   77
gift wrap   77
given name   4
glasses   38
gloves   79
go   18
go down   82
go out (to eat)   54
go up   82
golf   64
golf course   69
good   78
good time   92
gorgeous   113
grains   55
grandfather   28
grandmother   28

grandparent   28
grape   55
graphic designer   10
great   42
green   81
grilled   53
ground floor   82
guaranteed   46
guitar   64
guy   29
gym   68

H

hair dryer   44
hardly ever   68
have   30
have to   66
he   8
health   60
healthful   60
healthy   60
heavy   78
helicopter   109
hello   44
her (possessive adjective)   8
hers (possessive pronoun)   80
Hi   44
him   80
hip-hop music   25
his   8
history   88
hometown   12
hosiery   76
hot   78
hot sauce   57
hotel maid   118
hotel reservation   104
house   64
housework   36
how many   32
how much   116
how often   68
how old   8
hurry   101
husband   28

I

I   8
ice   53
important   77
in   18
in moderation   60
in shape   70

Social language list

This is a unit-by-unit list of all the productive social language from *Top Notch 1*.

Welcome to *Top Notch!*

Hi, my name's [Peter].
I'm [Alexandra].
Everyone calls me [Alex].
Good morning. / Good afternoon.
Good evening. / Good night.
What do you do?
I'm a [student]. And you?

[Alex], this is [Emily]. [Emily], this is [Alex].
Nice to meet you, [Emily].
Well, it was nice meeting you.
See you later.
Bye. / Good-bye.
Take it easy. / Take care.
What's this called in English?

That's right.
How do you say [your last name]?
What's your [last name], please?
I'm sorry. Could you repeat that?
Sure.
How do you spell [your first name]?
Thanks. / Thank you.

Unit 1

This is [my teacher].
Please call me [Tom].
Let me introduce you to [my wife, Carol].
Good to meet you.
Pleasure to meet you.
Are you [Bill]?

No, I'm [David].
That's [Bill] over there.
Are you [a student]?
As a matter of fact, [I am].
Is she from [São Paulo]?
Those are the [new students].
Who's that?

Come. I'll introduce you.
I'd like you to meet [Kate].
What's your name?
Where's he from?
How old are they?
Could you say that louder?

Unit 2

Do you want to see [a concert] on [Saturday]?
That's not for me.
I'm not really a [rock] fan.
What about [Sergio Mendes]?
Now that's more my style!
There's a [show] at [eleven thirty].
That's past my bedtime!
No problem.

Perfect.
See you then.
Are you free on [Friday]?
Really? (to show enthusiasm)
I'd love to go.
I'd love to go, but I'm busy on [Friday].
What time?
Too bad.
Maybe some other time.

When's the [concert]?
What time's the [movie]?
Where's the [play]?
Excuse me. (to get someone's attention)
I'm looking for [The Bell Theater].
That's right [around the corner], on the [left] side of the street.
I'm sorry, I'm not from around here.
Thanks, anyway.

Unit 3

What are you up to?
Come take a look.
Let me see.
Who's that [guy]? / Who are [those two]?
Really! (to show surprise)
Tell me something about [your family].
Sure.
What do you want to know?

Do you have any [brothers or sisters]?
I have [one younger sister].
Do they look like you?
Not really.
So what does [your sister] do?
That's great!
How about [your brother]?
How many [children] do you have?
How are you alike?

How are you different?
Do you look alike?
We wear similar clothes.
Do you both [like basketball]?
She [likes basketball], and I do too.
She doesn't [like fish], and I don't either.
He [likes coffee], but I don't.

Unit 4

This [printer] is driving me crazy!
It's not working.
It's just a lemon!
What do you mean?
What's wrong with it?
Hey, [Bob]! (as a greeting)
What are *you* doing here? (to express surprise)

I'm looking for [a laptop].
Any suggestions?
What about [a Pell]?
Really? (to ask for clarification)
How's it going?
Fine, thanks.
I'm sorry to hear that.
That's too bad. / That's a shame.

The [window] won't open / close.
The [iron] won't turn on / off.
The [fridge] is making a funny sound.
The [toilet] won't flush.
The [toilet] won't stop flushing.
The [sink] is clogged.
Hello? (to answer the telephone)
This is room [211]. Can I help you?

Unit 5

Are you ready to order?
Do you need some more time?
I think I'll start with [the soup].
Then I'll have [the chicken].
That comes with [salad], doesn't it?

There's a choice of vegetables.
Tonight we have [carrots].
Certainly.
Anything [to drink]? / And [to drink]?
What is there to [eat]?

Is that all?
I'm in the mood for [seafood].
Sorry. You're out of luck.
Let's go out!
Good idea!

I'll have the [pasta] for my [main course].
What does that come with?
What kind of [soup] is there?
I think I'll have the [salad].
What do you feel like eating [tonight]?
The [special] sounds delicious.

What about the [chicken]?
Sounds good.
Excuse me! (to get attention in a restaurant)
We're ready to order.
Would you like to start with [an appetizer]?

And for your [main course]?
We have [a nice seafood special] on the menu.
We'll take the check, please.
Is the tip included?
Do you accept credit cards?

Unit 6

Where are you off to?
I'm on my way to [the park].
Do you want to play together sometime?
That would be great.
No way.
He's a couch potato.
Too bad.

I'm crazy about [tennis].
Why don't we [play basketball] sometime?
Great idea.
When's good for you?
Sorry, I can't. (to express regret)
I have to [meet my sister at the airport].
That sounds great.

You too?
Actually, I usually go [in the evening].
How come?
Well, have a great time.
He's in shape / out of shape.
We don't eat junk food.
[They] avoid sweets.
[I have] a sweet tooth.

Unit 7

Excuse me. (to ask for assistance in a shop)
How much is that [V-neck] / are those [pants]?
That's not too bad.
Do you have it / them in [a larger size]?
It is / These are too [short].
Here you go.
Would you like to try it / them on?
No, thanks.

Would you be nice enough to [gift wrap it / them for me]?
Of course.
We have a pair in [brown].
See if they are better.
Let me see if I can find you something better.
Yes, they're fine.
I'll take the [loafers].
How would you like to pay for them?

Excuse me? (to ask for clarification)
Cash or charge?
Go straight.
Turn left / right.
Go down / up the stairs.
Take the escalator / elevator / stairs.
It's on the top / first / ground floor.
It's in the basement.
It's in the front / back.

Unit 8

When did you get back?
Just [yesterday].
Tell me about your trip.
I had a [really great] time.
I'll bet the [food] was [great].
Amazing! (to express delight)
How was the [flight]?
I was [pretty bumpy], actually.

Let me help you with your [things].
Thanks a lot.
Did you just get in?
My [flight] was [a little late].
Welcome back!
OK.
What did you do [last weekend]?
Nothing special.

What about you?
It was so [relaxing].
[The weather] was terrible.
[The people] were unfriendly.
They canceled [my flight].
Someone stole [my wallet].

Unit 9

Do you speak [English]?
I'm looking for [the bullet train].
Which one?
I'm taking that, too.
You can follow me.
It leaves from [track 15].
We should hurry.
By the way, where are you from?
No kidding!

What a small world!
Can we make the [2:00 bus]?
It left / departed [five minutes] ago.
Oh, no!
What should we do?
One way or round-trip?
I'm going to need [a rental car] in [Dubai].
What date are you arriving?

What time do you get in?
Let me check.
We had an accident / mechanical problems.
We missed our [train].
We got bumped from the flight.
We got seasick.

Unit 10

I'm almost out of cash.
Let's go in here.
What about this?
It's a bit more than I want to spend.
Maybe you could get a better price.
You think so?
It can't hurt to ask.
How much can you spend?

No more than [amount].
Could I have a look?
How much do you want for [that rug]?
This one?
The other one.
I can give you [amount].
That sounds fair.
This jacket is a bargain.

I'm sorry. That's just too much for me.
Pretty good!
What a great deal!
What a rip-off!
She got a good price.
She saved a lot of money.
He paid too much.

Pronunciation table

These are the pronunciation symbols used in *Top Notch 1*.

Vowels	
Symbol	Key Words
i	b**ea**t, f**ee**d
ɪ	b**i**t, d**i**d
eɪ	d**a**te, p**ai**d
ɛ	b**e**t, b**e**d
æ	b**a**t, b**a**d
ɑ	b**o**x, **o**dd, f**a**ther
ɔ	b**ou**ght, d**o**g
oʊ	b**oa**t, r**oa**d
ʊ	b**oo**k, g**oo**d
u	b**oo**t, f**oo**d, fl**u**
ʌ	b**u**t, m**u**d, m**o**ther
ə	b**a**n**a**na, **a**mong
ɚ	sh**ir**t, m**ur**der
aɪ	b**i**te, c**r**y, b**uy**, **eye**
aʊ	ab**out**, h**ow**
ɔɪ	v**oi**ce, b**oy**
ɪr	d**eer**
ɛr	b**are**
ɑr	b**ar**
ɔr	d**oor**
ʊr	t**our**

Consonants			
Symbol	Key Words	Symbol	Key Words
p	**p**ack, ha**pp**y	z	**z**ip, plea**s**e, goe**s**
b	**b**ack, ru**bb**er	ʃ	**sh**ip, ma**ch**ine, sta**ti**on, spe**ci**al, discu**ss**ion
t	**t**ie		
d	**d**ie	ʒ	mea**s**ure, vi**s**ion
k	**c**ame, **k**ey, **qu**ick	h	**h**ot, **wh**o
g	**g**ame, **g**uest	m	**m**en
tʃ	**ch**urch, na**t**ure, wa**tch**	n	su**n**, **kn**ow, **pn**eumonia
dʒ	**j**udge, **g**eneral, ma**j**or	ŋ	su**ng**, ri**ng**ing
f	**f**an, photogra**ph**	w	**w**et, **wh**ite
v	**v**an	l	**l**ight, **l**ong
θ	**th**ing, brea**th**	r	**r**ight, **wr**ong
ð	**th**en, brea**th**e	y	**y**es
s	**s**ip, **c**ity, p**s**ychology		
t̬	bu**tt**er, bo**tt**le		
tˀ	bu**tt**on		

Non-count nouns

This list is an at-a-glance reference to the non-count nouns used in *Top Notch 1*.

aerobics	candy	dancing	fruit	ice	music	running	sightseeing	traffic
air-conditioning	cash	dessert	golf	juice	nature	salad	skydiving	transportation
basketball	cheese	dinner	grain	junk food	oil	salt	sleepwear	TV
beef	chicken	electronics	health	lamb	outerwear	sausage	soccer	walking
bike riding	clothing	English	history	lettuce	pasta	seafood	soup	water
bread	coffee	entertainment	hosiery	lingerie	pepper	service	squid	weather
broccoli	crab	fish	hot sauce	meat	pie	shopping	swimming	wildlife
butter	culture	food	housework	milk	rice	shrimp	tennis	yogurt
cake								

Irregular verbs

base form	simple past	past participle	base form	simple past	past participle	base form	simple past	past participle
be	was / were	been	get	got	gotten	see	saw	seen
begin	began	begun	give	gave	given	sell	sold	sold
break	broke	broken	go	went	gone	send	sent	sent
bring	brought	brought	grow	grew	grown	sing	sang	sung
build	built	built	have	had	had	sit	sat	sat
buy	bought	bought	hear	heard	heard	sleep	slept	slept
catch	caught	caught	hit	hit	hit	speak	spoke	spoken
choose	chose	chosen	hurt	hurt	hurt	spend	spent	spent
come	came	come	keep	kept	kept	stand	stood	stood
cost	cost	cost	know	knew	knew	steal	stole	stolen
cut	cut	cut	leave	left	left	swim	swam	swum
do	did	done	lose	lost	lost	take	took	taken
drink	drank	drunk	make	made	made	teach	taught	taught
drive	drove	driven	mean	meant	meant	tell	told	told
eat	ate	eaten	meet	met	met	think	thought	thought
fall	fell	fallen	pay	paid	paid	throw	threw	thrown
find	found	found	put	put	put	understand	understood	understood
fit	fit	fit	quit	quit	quit	wake up	woke up	woken up
fly	flew	flown	read	read	read	wear	wore	worn
fall	fell	fallen	ride	rode	ridden	win	won	won
feel	felt	felt	run	run	run	write	wrote	written
forget	forgot	forgotten	say	said	said			

GRAMMAR BOOSTER

The *Grammar Booster* is optional. It provides more explanation and practice, as well as additional grammar concepts.

UNIT 1 Lesson 1

Verb be : usage

Use the verb be to give information about the subject of a sentence. The subject of a sentence can be a noun or a pronoun.

noun subject	pronoun subject
The **teacher** is Chinese.	**We**'re Peruvian.

Verb be: forms

Affirmative statements

There are three forms of the verb be in the present tense: am, are, and is.

I **am** a student.   We **are** married.
You **are** late.   They **are** Canadian.
He
She **is** in the room.
It

Contracted forms

In speaking and informal writing, contract be with subject nouns and pronouns.

I am a student.	=	**I'm** a student.	**He is** in the room.	=	**He's** in the room.
You are late.	=	**You're** late.	**Peter is** a singer.	=	**Peter's** a singer.

Negative contractions

There are two ways to contract in negative sentences.

He's not Brazilian. OR **He isn't** Brazilian.   **They're not** teachers. OR **They aren't** teachers.

Note: There's only one kind of negative contraction for I am not: I'm not.

Verb be: yes / no questions; affirmative and negative short answers

It's common to answer yes / no questions with short answers (or just Yes or No). Don't use contractions with affirmative short answers.

yes / no question	affirmative	negative
Are you a salesperson?	Yes, I am. NOT ~~Yes I'm~~.	No, I'm not.
Is he Italian?	Yes, he is. NOT ~~Yes he's~~.	No, he's not / he isn't.
Are they students?	Yes, they are. NOT ~~Yes they're~~.	No, they're not / they aren't.

A Choose an answer for each question.

_____	**1.** Are they Chinese?	**a.** Yes, it is.
_____	**2.** Are you hungry?	**b.** No, I'm not.
_____	**3.** Is he a teacher?	**c.** No, she isn't.
_____	**4.** Is she Russian?	**d.** Yes, they are.
_____	**5.** Am I in your class?	**e.** Yes, he is.
_____	**6.** Is it 3:00?	**f.** Yes, you are.

B Answer the questions with short answers.

1. Is Tokyo in China? _No, it isn't_ .
2. Is Spanish easy? _Yes, it is_ .
3. Are cats animals? _Yes the are_ .

4. Is Paris a country? _No, it isn't_ .
5. Are you a musician? _No, I am not_ .
6. Are Korea and Japan in Asia? _Yes, the are_ .

UNIT 1 Lesson 2

Information questions with be

Use <u>Who</u> to ask about people, <u>What</u> to ask about things, <u>Where</u> to ask about places, and <u>How old</u> to ask about age.

singular nouns	plural nouns
Who's your teacher?	**Who are** the new students?
What's your name?	**What are** their names?
Where is your father from?	**Where are** your classmates from?
How old is your sister?	**How old are** your children?

Possessive nouns and possessive adjectives

Possessive nouns

Add 's to a name or a noun.

Where is **Mary's** father from?   What's your **mother's** name?

Add an apostrophe (') to plural nouns that end in -s.

What are the **students'** names?

Possessive adjectives

Where's Mary's father from? → Where's **her** father from?
What's Emilio's last name? → What's **his** last name?
What's Lee and Gan's address? → What's **their** address?

A Choose an answer for each question.

___e___ 1. What's your name?
_____ 2. Where is he from?
_____ 3. Where's her mother from?
_____ 4. Who are they?
_____ 5. How old are your cousins?

a. Wales, actually. He's British.
b. Kwon-su and Toshinaga.
c. Sasha's mother? San Francisco, I think.
d. Twelve and ten.
e. I'm Milos. But everyone calls me Mishka.

B Write questions with <u>What</u> and a possessive adjective.

1. A: _What's their address_ ?
   B: Lin and Ben's? It's 2 Bay St.

2. A: _____ ?
   B: His phone number? It's 21-66-55.

3. A: _____ ?
   B: Dave's last name? It's Bourne.

4. A: _____ ?
   B: Sandra's nickname is Sandy.

5. A: _____ ?
   B: Our number? Oh, it's 555 298-0093.

6. A: _____ ?
   B: Ray's? His address is 456 Rue Noire.

UNIT 2 Lesson 1

Prepositions of time and place

Time

Use <u>on</u> with the names of days or dates.

on Thursday	on Monday morning	on New Year's Day
on the weekend	on Sundays	on a weekday

Use <u>in</u> with periods of time (but not with names of days).

in 1998	in July	in [the] spring
in the morning	in the 20th century	in the 1950s

Use <u>at</u> with specific moments in time.

at 9:00	at ten thirty-five	at 6 o'clock
at sunrise	at noon	at midnight

Place

Use <u>on</u> with the names of streets and specific physical locations.

on Main Street	on Smith Avenue	on the corner
on the street	on the right	on the left

Use <u>in</u> with the names of cities, countries, continents, and other large locations.

in the neighborhood	in the center of town	in Caracas
in Thailand	in Africa	in the ocean

Use <u>at</u> for buildings and addresses.

at the theater	at the supermarket	at the bank
at the train station	at 10 Main Street	at 365 Smith Avenue

A ▷ **Complete each sentence or question with <u>on</u>, <u>in</u>, or <u>at</u>.**

1. When's the movie? The movie is _____ Friday _____ 8:30.

2. _____ the weekend, I'm going to the concert _____ the public library.

3. Where is he? He's not here right now. He's _____ work.

4. Where's his office? It's _____ the center of town.

5. When was her mother born? She was born _____ January 1.

6. When does the movie take place? It takes place _____ the 19th century _____ Africa.

7. There is a ticket booth _____ the center of town.

8. Is the concert hall _____ Grove Street?

9. I think the theater is _____ the right side of the street.

10. Let's go to the early show. The concert is outside, and the weather gets really hot _____ the afternoon.

11. This concert occurs every second year _____ November.

12. I'll see you _____ Thursday morning in front of the theater, OK?

1.

★ METRO ★
HILL STREET MALL
8:55PM   Friday, Oct. 17
Phantom of the Opera

2.

ELECTRIC MAYHEM
MIDNIGHT CONCERT
THE CAT CLUB
SAT. OCTOBER 23 $18

questions: _____

_____

answers: _____

_____

questions: _____

_____

answers: _____

_____

UNIT 3 Lesson 1

The simple present tense: usage

Use the simple present tense to talk about facts and habitual actions in the present.

facts	habitual actions
Hank **speaks** French very well.	I **go** to bed at 10:00 p.m. every night.
I **work** at 43 Fork Road.	She **eats** lunch at Safi's Cafe on Fridays.

The simple present tense: form

Add **–s** to the base form of the verb for third-person singular (<u>he</u>, <u>she</u>, <u>it</u>).

I **like** Japanese food.	He **likes** Mexican food.
You **study** Korean.	She **studies** English.
They **open** at 7:00.	It **opens** at 8:00.
We **work** at a restaurant.	

Use <u>don't</u> (do not) and <u>doesn't</u> (does not) and the base form of the verb to make negative statements.

I **don't go** to bed before 10:00 p.m.   Hank **doesn't speak** Spanish very well.

The simple present tense: <u>yes</u> / <u>no</u> questions

Use <u>do</u> or <u>does</u> and the base form to make <u>yes</u> / <u>no</u> questions in the simple present tense.

Do you **speak** Portuguese?   **Does** she **live** near you?   (NOT ~~Does she lives near you?~~)

A Write negative sentences.

1. Hank likes jazz. (His brother) *His brother doesn't like jazz* _____ .

2. Vic lives in Lima. (His sisters) _____ .

3. Kate works in a hospital. (Her sister) _____ .

4. My sister has a big family. (My brother) _____ .

5. My older brother speaks Japanese. (My younger brother) _____ .

6. Han's niece takes a bus to school. (His nephew) _____ .

B ▷ Practice. Write <u>yes</u> / <u>no</u> questions.

1. ___*Does your brother*___ drink coffee? No, he doesn't. My brother drinks tea.

2. _____ sister? Yes, I do. I really look like my sister.

3. _____ children? No, we don't have any yet.

4. _____ in Chile? No, my in-laws live in Argentina.

5. _____ English? Yes, she does. My niece speaks it very well.

▶ UNIT 3 Lesson 2

┌─ **The simple present tense: form of information questions** ─────────

Use <u>do</u> or <u>does</u> and the base form of the verb to ask information questions.

Where do your in-laws **live**?   **What does** your sister **do**?
When do you **visit** your parents?   **What time does** she **go**?

Don't use <u>do</u> or <u>does</u> with <u>Who</u>. Always use the third-person singular to ask information questions with <u>Who</u> in the simple present tense.

Who lives here? My parents **do**.

Use <u>How many</u> with plural nouns.

How many children **do** you **have**?   **How many** books **does** she **have**?
How many aunts and uncles **do** you **have**?   **How many** languages **does** he **speak**?

└──

A ▷ Complete the questions.

1. _____ your father _____? He's a doctor.

2. _____ your grandparents _____? They live in Seoul.

3. _____ children _____? I have two boys and three girls.

4. _____ your in-laws? We visit them on Sundays.

5. _____ your brother _____? He lives across the street from me.

6. _____ speaks French? My uncle does.

7. _____ you _____? I study early in the morning at around 7:00.

8. _____ has four children? My cousins do.

9. _____ your son _____ breakfast? He eats breakfast at 8:00.

▶ UNIT 4 Lesson 1

┌─ **The present continuous: spelling rules** ─────────

To form a present participle, add <u>–ing</u> to the base form of the verb.

talk → talk**ing**

If the base form ends in a silent (unvoiced) <u>–e</u>, drop the <u>–e</u> and add <u>–ing</u>.

leave → leav**ing**

└──

In verbs of one syllable, if the last three letters are a consonant-vowel-consonant*
sequence, double the last consonant and then add **–ing** to the base form.

    C   V   C

    s   i   t → si**tt**ing

BUT: If the verb ends in –w, –x, or –y, don't double the final consonant.

    blow → **blowing**

    fix → **fixing**

    say → **saying**

In verbs of more than one syllable that end in a consonant-vowel-consonant sequence,
double the last consonant only if the spoken stress is on the last syllable.

    permít → permi**tt**ing   BUT órder → ordering

*Vowels = a, e, i, o, u
Consonants = b, c, d, f, g, h, j, k, l, m, n, p, q, r, s, t, v, w, x, y, z

 A   **Write the present participle for the following base forms.**

1. turn	*turning*	**7.** stop	_____	**13.** sew	_____	**19.** change	_____
2. rain	_____	**8.** exit	_____	**14.** listen	_____	**20.** be	_____
3. run	_____	**9.** sit	_____	**15.** do	_____	**21.** have	_____
4. help	_____	**10.** eat	_____	**16.** write	_____	**22.** put	_____
5. open	_____	**11.** buy	_____	**17.** begin	_____	**23.** go	_____
6. close	_____	**12.** mix	_____	**18.** use	_____		

The present continuous: statements

Form the present continuous with a form of **be** and the present participle.

affirmative statements	negative statements
I**'m studying** English.	I**'m** not **studying** French.
You**'re studying** French.	You**'re** not **studying** English.
He**'s reading** a book.	He**'s** not **reading** a newspaper.
She**'s reading** a newspaper.	She**'s** not **reading** a book.
We**'re watching** TV.	We**'re** not **watching** a video.
They**'re watching** a video.	They**'re** not **watching** TV.

B   **Change each affirmative statement to a negative statement. Use contractions.**

1. She's going to the supermarket. _____.

2. He's calling his wife this afternoon. _____.

3. I'm buying tickets for a rock concert tonight. _____.

4. The Roberts are feeding their kids early. _____.

5. Jack is taking the bus to the movies. _____.

C   **Write answers to the questions.**

1. Are you studying English this year? _____.

2. When are you taking a vacation? _____.

3. Is it raining now? _____.

4. Where are you eating dinner tonight? _____.

5. Are you listening to music now? _____.

The present continuous: questions

Yes / no questions: Place <u>be</u> before the subject of the sentence.

Is she watching TV?   **Are we** meeting this afternoon?
Are you driving there?   **Are they** talking on the phone?

Information questions: Use question words to ask information questions.

When are you going?   **Who**'s talking on the phone?
What are you doing right now?   **Why** are you buying that pocket translator?

D Complete each conversation with a question in the present continuous.

1. A: _____?
   B: No. Evan's not watching TV right now.

2. A: _____?
   B: Yes, she's working this morning.

3. A: _____?
   B: I'm calling Janet Hammond.

4. A: _____?
   B: She's coming home later tonight.

UNIT 5 *Lesson 1*

Non-count nouns: categories and verb agreement

Non-count nouns are common in the following categories:

    abstract ideas: health, advice, help, luck, fun
    sports and activities: tennis, swimming, golf, basketball
    illnesses: cancer, AIDS, diabetes, dengue
    natural events: rain, snow, wind, light, darkness
    academic subjects: English, chemistry, art, mathematics
    foods: rice, milk, sugar, coffee, fat

All non-count nouns require a singular verb.

    Fat **isn't** good for you.
    Mathematics **is** my favorite subject.

A Complete each sentence with the correct form of the verb.

1. Coffee _____ my favorite beverage.
       be

2. Rice _____ very good for you, even when you are sick.
       be

3. Influenza _____ pain and fever.
       cause

4. Mathematics _____ problems for many students, but not for me!
       create

5. Darkness _____ some people, but I don't know why.
       frighten

6. Medical advice _____ people answer questions about their health.
       help

B ▷ Complete each statement with a countable quantity. (Note: More than one phrase of quantity may be possible.)

liquids

1. This soup is too salty. It has _a cup of_ salt in it!

2. She must be very thirsty. This is her third _____ water.

3. My car has a big gas tank. It holds _____ gas.

solids

4. I ate _____ cheese and now I feel sick.

5. A club sandwich doesn't have two _____ bread. It has three _____ bread.

6. I like my tea sweet. Please put in _____ sugar.

C ▷ Complete each question with **How much** or **How many**.

1. _____ bread do we need? I put two loaves in the shopping cart.

2. _____ salt did you put in the beef stew? I can't eat it.

3. _____ hot pepper do you like? This food is already very spicy!

4. _____ spoonfuls of sugar do you want in your tea? Two, please.

5. _____ oil should I put in this salad? A half cup?

6. _____ cheese is there in the kitchen? I think we need to get some more.

7. _____ slices of bread do you want? Only one, thanks.

8. _____ cups of coffee did you drink? Your hands are shaking!

Plural count nouns: spelling rules

Add –s to most nouns.

cup	**cups**		appetizer	**appetizers**
apple	**apples**			

If a noun ends in a consonant and –y, change the y to i and add –es.

cherry	**cherries**		berry	**berries**

Add –es to nouns that end in –ch, –o, –s, –sh, –x, or –z.

lunch	**lunches**		radish	**radishes**
tomato	**tomatoes**		box	**boxes**
glass	**glasses**			

But do not change the y when the letter before the y is a vowel.

boy	**boys**

D ▷ Write the plural form of the following count nouns.

1. clam _____   5. spoonful _____   9. vegetable _____

2. slice _____   6. pear _____   10. potato _____

3. cup _____   7. french fry _____

4. olive _____   8. sandwich _____

UNIT 5 Lesson 2

A ▷ Write a or an. If the noun is a non-count noun, write X.

1. He has _____ diabetes.

2. She would like to eat _____ pear.

3. "_____ apple a day keeps the doctor away."

4. Would you like _____ appetizer?

5. There's _____ egg on the shelf.

6. Does the restaurant serve _____ rice with the chicken?

7. We'd like _____ water, please.

8. He always gives _____ good advice.

9. Let's go to _____ concert tonight.

10. My family loves _____ music.

Some and any

Use some and any to describe an indefinite number or amount.

There are **some** apples in the fridge. (Indefinite number: we don't know how many.)
Are there **any** oranges? (Indefinite number: no specific number being asked about.)
They are bringing us **some** coffee. (Indefinite amount: we don't know how much.)
Now we have **some**. (Indefinite amount: we don't know how much.)

Use some with non-count nouns and with plural count nouns in affirmative statements.

      non-count noun   plural count noun
We need **some** milk and **some** bananas. (affirmative statement)

Use any with non-count nouns and plural count nouns in negative statements.

      non-count noun   plural count noun
We don't want **any** cheese, and we don't need **any** apples.
They don't have **any**.

Use any or some in questions with count and non-count nouns.

Do you need **any** cookies or butter?
Do you need **some** cookies or butter?

Change the following sentences from affirmative to negative.

1. There is some coffee in the kitchen.
   <u>There isn't any coffee in the kitchen</u>.

2. There are some beans on the table.
   _____.

3. We have some leftovers.
   _____.

4. They need some onions for the soup.
   _____.

5. She's buying some fruit at the market.
   _____.

6. The Reeds want some eggs for breakfast.
   _____.

7. I want some butter on my sandwich.
   _____.

8. There is some chicken in the fridge.
   _____.

9. They need some cheese for the pasta.
   _____.

C **Complete each statement with some or any.**

1. I don't want _____ more coffee, thank you.

2. There isn't _____ salt in this soup.

3. We don't see _____ sandwiches on the menu.

4. They need _____ sugar for their tea.

5. The restaurant is making _____ cakes for the party.

6. It's too bad that there isn't _____ soup.

7. I don't see _____ menus on those tables.

8. There are _____ eggs for the omelet.

UNIT 6 Lesson 1

Can: form

Use can with the base form of a verb.

She **can play** golf very well.
NOT She ~~cans play~~ golf very well.
NOT She ~~can plays~~ golf very well.
NOT She ~~can to play~~ golf very well.

There are three negative forms of can.

He **can't** swim.   =   He **cannot** swim.   =   He **can not** swim.

A **Correct the following sentences.**

1. Can you ~~coming~~ ^{come} to the party next week?

2. My brother-in-law can't plays basketball tomorrow.

3. I'm going to the pool with Diane, but I no can swim.

4. Alice can to go running after work.

5. Can Lisa visits her cousins next weekend?

Can: information questions

Where **can** I go running around here?	Try the park.
When **can** you **come** for dinner?	How about tomorrow night?
How often **can** you **go** running?	No more than twice a week. I'm pretty busy.
What languages **can** you **speak**?	I can speak Italian.
Who **can drive**?	I can.

 B **Complete the questions, using can.**

1. **A:** _____ aerobics around here? (Where / I / do)
   B: Why don't you try Total Fitness? They have great instructors.

2. **A:** _____ English together? (When / we / study)
   B: Let's get together tomorrow night. OK?

3. **A:** We need some fresh air. _____ walking? (Where / we / go)
   B: Well, we can go over to Grant Park. It's very nice.

4. **A:** _____ golf? (How often / Larry / play)
   B: Not very often. He's starting a new job.

5. **A:** _____ dinner tonight? (Who / make)
   B: What about Katherine? She's not doing anything.

Have to: form

Use have to or has to with the base form of a verb. Use has to for the third-person singular.

I **have to go** to class at 9:00.
She **has to go** to class at 8:00.
NOT She ~~has to goes~~ to class at 8:00.
NOT She ~~has to going~~ to class at 8:00.

C **Correct these sentences.**

1. My brother-in-law ~~have~~ *has* to work on the weekend.

2. Do you has to meet Mr. Green at the airport?

3. We don't have to making dinner tonight. We're going out.

4. Ms. Davis has to fills out an application for her English class.

5. Does she have to watches TV now? I'm trying to study.

Have to: information questions

What does he **have to do** Saturday morning?	He has to clean the house.
How often does she **have to work** on the weekend?	Not often.
When do they **have to go** shopping?	Tonight. The party's tomorrow.
Who **has to write** the report?	Marian.
Where do you **have to go** this morning?	To the airport.

D **Complete the questions.**

1. **A:** _____ she _____ do tomorrow?
   B: She has to go to English class.

2. **A:** _____ he _____ take the medicine?
   B: Every three hours.

3. **A:** _____ she _____ go to the park?
   B: At around eight.

4. **A:** _____ they _____ do after class?
   B: Nothing special.

5. **A:** _____ we _____ turn off the machine?
   B: Never! Don't ever turn it off.

6. **A:** _____ you _____ pick up your sister?
   B: At about two thirty.

UNIT 6 Lesson 2

The simple present tense: non-action verbs

Some verbs are non-action verbs. Most non-action verbs are not usually used in the present continuous, even when they are describing a situation that is happening right now.

    I **want** a sandwich. NOT ~~I'm wanting a sandwich.~~

Some common non-action verbs:

    be   have   know   like   love   miss   need   see   understand   want

Some non-action verbs have action and non-action meanings.

non-action meaning	action meaning
I **have** two sandwiches. (possession)	**I'm having** a sandwich. (eating)
I **think** English is difficult. (opinion)	**I'm thinking** about her. (the act of thinking)

A **Write the verbs in the simple present tense or the present continuous.**

Dear Kevin,

    It's 2:00 and I _____ of you. The kids _____ outside. I _____
             1. think   2. play   3. see
them through the window right now. They _____ a small table and chairs and
                                  4. have
they _____ a late lunch.
    5. have
    I _____ to mail this letter before the post office closes. I _____ you're
       6. want   7. know
working hard and we all _____ you.
                  8. miss
Maggie

The simple present tense: frequency adverbs

Frequency adverbs generally follow forms of the verb **be** and precede all other verbs.

be	frequency adverb	
I **'m**	**usually**	at the pool on Saturdays.

frequency adverb	verb	
I **usually**	**go**	to the pool on Saturdays.

Sometimes, usually, often, generally, and occasionally can also go at the beginning or the end of a sentence. Don't use the other frequency adverbs there.

    Sometimes I go to the pool on Sundays.
    I go to the pool **often**.
    NOT Never I go to the pool. OR I go to the pool never.

In negative sentences, most frequency adverbs can precede OR follow <u>don't</u> or <u>doesn't</u>.

Hank **usually** doesn't go running on the weekend.
Hank doesn't **usually** go running on the weekend.

But note that <u>always</u> CANNOT precede <u>don't</u> or <u>doesn't</u>.

I don't **always** have breakfast in the morning.
NOT I ~~always don't have~~ breakfast in the morning.

Don't use <u>never</u> with a negative verb. Use the frequency adverb <u>ever</u> with negative verbs.

I **never** eat sweets.   =   I **don't ever** eat sweets.
NOT I ~~don't never~~ eat sweets.

The simple present tense: time expressions

Time expressions generally go at the beginning or the end of a sentence.

I go to the pool **three times a week**.   **Three times a week**, I go to the pool.

The time expression <u>a lot</u> can appear only at the end of a sentence.

I go to the pool **a lot**.   NOT ~~A lot I go to the pool.~~

some time expressions
every week
every other day
once a month
twice a year
three times a week
other expressions
once in a while
a lot

B These sentences are not written correctly. Rewrite them correctly.

1. She plays usually golf on Sunday.

   _____.

2. They go to the park hardly ever.

   _____.

3. I always am hungry in the afternoon.

   _____.

4. We once in a while have eggs for breakfast.

   _____.

5. Pat doesn't never exercise.

   _____.

6. Never I go swimming at night.

   _____.

7. Victor doesn't drink always coffee.

   _____.

8. Connie and I play twice a week tennis together.

   _____.

9. We go often bike riding in the afternoon.

   _____.

10. She is every day late for class.

   _____.

UNIT 7 Lesson 1

Comparative forms of adjectives

Add **–er** to one-syllable adjectives. If the adjective ends in **–e**, add **–r**.

cheap → cheap**er**   loose → loos**er**

If an adjective ends consonant-vowel-consonant, double the final consonant before adding **–er**.

hot → ho**tt**er

For most adjectives that end in **–y**, change the **y** to **i** and add **–er**.

pretty → prett**ier**   busy → bus**ier**

To make the comparative form of most adjectives of two or more syllables, use <u>more</u> or <u>less</u>.

She's **less practical** than her sister.   DVDs are **more popular** than videos.

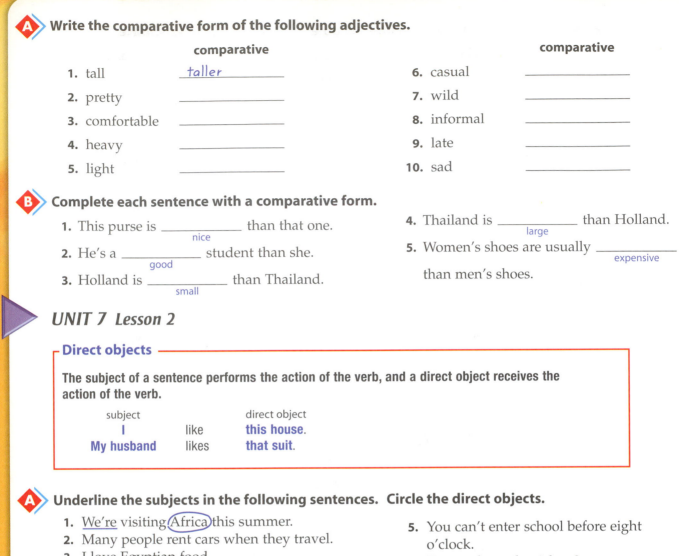

A Write the comparative form of the following adjectives.

comparative

1. tall   _taller_

2. pretty   _____

3. comfortable   _____

4. heavy   _____

5. light   _____

comparative

6. casual   _____

7. wild   _____

8. informal   _____

9. late   _____

10. sad   _____

B Complete each sentence with a comparative form.

1. This purse is _____ than that one.

nice

2. He's a _____ student than she.

good

3. Holland is _____ than Thailand.

small

4. Thailand is _____ than Holland.

large

5. Women's shoes are usually _____

expensive

than men's shoes.

UNIT 7 Lesson 2

Direct objects

The subject of a sentence performs the action of the verb, and a direct object receives the action of the verb.

subject		direct object
I	like	**this house**.
My husband	likes	**that suit**.

A Underline the subjects in the following sentences. Circle the direct objects.

1. We're visiting Africa this summer.
2. Many people rent cars when they travel.
3. I love Egyptian food.
4. Sanford and Mary never eat meat.
5. You can't enter school before eight o'clock.
6. Do you have the tickets?
7. Marie wants coffee with cream.

Indirect objects

When a sentence contains a direct object and prepositional phrase, you can use an indirect object to say the same thing.

prepositional phrase
I'm buying the gloves **for her**.
Give the sweater **to Ben**.

indirect object
I'm buying **her** the gloves.
Give **Ben** the sweater.

B Rewrite each sentence, changing the prepositional phrase into an indirect object.

1. She buys groceries for us. _She buys us groceries_____.

2. Laura sends a check to them every month. _____.

3. At night we read stories to them. _____.

4. They serve meals to us in the dining room. _____.

5. They never give gifts to me on my birthday. _____.

C Rewrite each sentence, changing each indirect object into a prepositional phrase.

1. He always gives me a check when I ask. _He always gives a check to me when I ask_ .

2. I send them the tickets and they give me a receipt. _____ .

3. Michael's assistant shows him the phone messages every day after lunch.

_____ .

D Add the indirect object or prepositional phrase to each sentence. Don't add words.

to me **1.** They send it on Monday. _They send it to me on Monday_ .

you **2.** Do they give breakfast on the tour? _____?

her **3.** We always tell the truth. _____ .

for him **4.** They make extra time. _____ .

UNIT 8 Lesson 1

The past tense of <u>be</u>: form

Use <u>was</u> or <u>were</u> for affirmative statements. Use <u>wasn't</u> or <u>weren't</u> for negative statements.

I **was** there yesterday.   They **were** there, too.
She **wasn't** my teacher.   They **weren't** my classmates.

The past tense of <u>be</u>: questions

Begin <u>yes</u> / <u>no</u> questions with <u>Was</u> or <u>Were</u>.

Was your flight on time?   **Were** you late?

Begin information questions with a question word followed by <u>was</u> or <u>were</u>.

How long was the flight?   **Where were** your passports?

A Complete the conversations with <u>was</u>, <u>were</u>, <u>wasn't</u>, or <u>weren't</u>.

1. **A:** _____ you out of town last week?

   B: No, I _____. Why?

   A: Well, you _____ at work, so I wasn't sure.

2. **A:** How _____ the food?

   B: Incredible! There _____ lots of fresh seafood and the fruit _____ delicious.

3. **A:** So _____ your vacation OK?

   B: Well, actually it _____. The food _____ terrible and the people _____ unfriendly. What more can I say?

4. **A:** Where _____ you last weekend?

   B: I _____ on vacation.

   A: Really? How _____ it?

5. **A:** How long _____ your vacation?

   B: Only a week. But you know something? After a week, the kids and I _____ pretty tired.

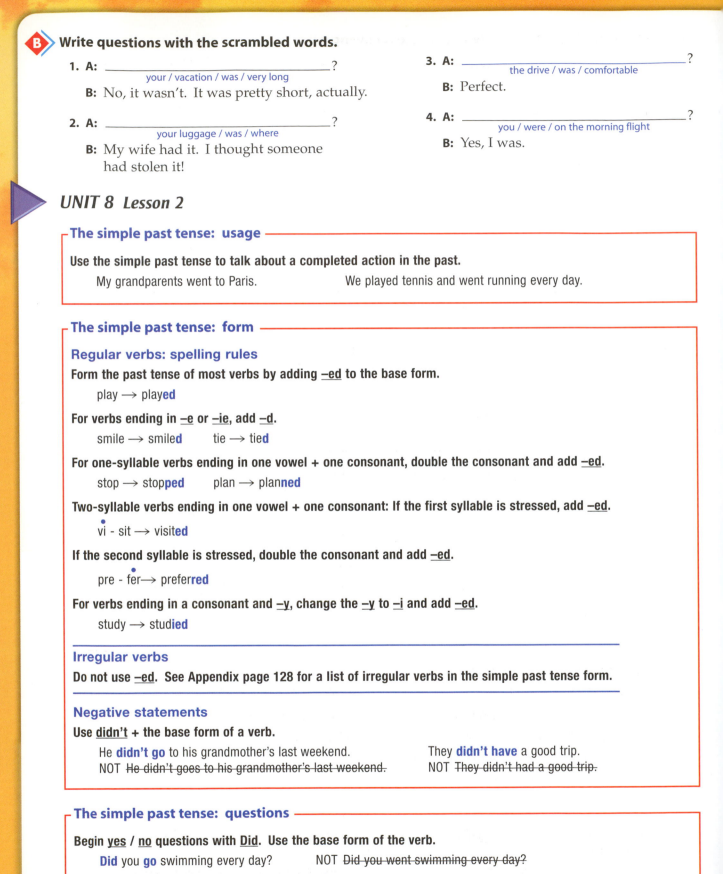

B **Write questions with the scrambled words.**

1. A: _____?
   your / vacation / was / very long

   B: No, it wasn't. It was pretty short, actually.

2. A: _____?
   your luggage / was / where

   B: My wife had it. I thought someone had stolen it!

3. A: _____?
   the drive / was / comfortable

   B: Perfect.

4. A: _____?
   you / were / on the morning flight

   B: Yes, I was.

UNIT 8 Lesson 2

The simple past tense: usage

Use the simple past tense to talk about a completed action in the past.

My grandparents went to Paris.   We played tennis and went running every day.

The simple past tense: form

Regular verbs: spelling rules

Form the past tense of most verbs by adding –ed to the base form.

play → play**ed**

For verbs ending in –e or –ie, add –d.

smile → smile**d**   tie → tie**d**

For one-syllable verbs ending in one vowel + one consonant, double the consonant and add –ed.

stop → stop**ped**   plan → plan**ned**

Two-syllable verbs ending in one vowel + one consonant: If the first syllable is stressed, add –ed.

vi - sit → visit**ed**

If the second syllable is stressed, double the consonant and add –ed.

pre - fer→ prefer**red**

For verbs ending in a consonant and –y, change the –y to –i and add –ed.

study → stud**ied**

Irregular verbs

Do not use –ed. See Appendix page 128 for a list of irregular verbs in the simple past tense form.

Negative statements

Use didn't + the base form of a verb.

He **didn't go** to his grandmother's last weekend.   They **didn't have** a good trip.
NOT He didn't goes to his grandmother's last weekend.   NOT They didn't had a good trip.

The simple past tense: questions

Begin yes / no questions with Did. Use the base form of the verb.

Did you **go** swimming every day?   NOT Did you went swimming every day?

Begin information questions with a question word followed by did.

Where did you go shopping?   **When did** you leave?   **What did** you eat everyday?

A ▷ **Write the simple past tense form of the following verbs.**

1. return _returned_
2. like _____
3. change _____
4. cry _____

5. try _____
6. stay _____
7. travel _____
8. arrive _____

9. rain _____
10. wait _____
11. offer _____
12. hurry _____

B ▷ **Write the simple past tense form of these irregular verbs.**

1. eat _ate_
2. drink _____
3. swim _____
4. go _____

5. write _____
6. meet _____
7. run _____
8. begin _____

9. buy _____
10. read _____
11. pay _____
12. understand _____

C ▷ **Complete the conversations with questions in the simple past tense.**
Use a capital letter to begin sentences.

1. **A:** _Where did you go on vacation last summer_ ?
   you / go / where / on vacation last summer
   B: We went to the mountains. It was very nice.

2. **A:** _____ ?
   you / get back / when / from vacation
   B: We got back last week. I'm sorry we didn't call you.

3. **A:** _____ ?
   they / have / a good flight
   B: Well, they said it was really scenic. So I guess so.

4. **A:** _____ ?
   you / do / what / in London
   B: We went to see some plays and we visited a few museums.

5. **A:** _____ ?
   your parents / enjoy / their trip
   B: Well, almost. There were some problems, but I think they had a good time.

UNIT 9 Lesson 1

Modals can, should, could: meaning

Use can to express ability or possibility.

Jerome **can** speak Korean.   **Can** you be there before 8:00?

Use could to suggest an alternative or to make a weak suggestion.

They **could** see an old movie like *Titanic*, or they **could** go to something new.

Use should to give advice or to express criticism.

You **should** think before you speak.

Modals: form

Modals are followed by the base form of the main verb of the sentence, except in short answers to questions.

Who **should read** this?   They **should**.   **Can** you **see** the moon tonight?   Yes, I **can**.

Never add –s to the third-person singular form of modals.

He **should** buy a ticket in advance.   NOT He shoulds buy a ticket in advance.

Never use to between modals and the base form.

You **could take** the train or the bus.   NOT ~~You could to take the train or the bus.~~

Use not between the modal and the base form.

You **shouldn't stay** at the Galaxy Hotel.   They **can't take** the express.

Modals: questions

In yes / no questions, the modal comes before the subject. In information questions, the question word precedes the modal.

yes / no questions

Should I buy a round-trip ticket?
Can we make the 1:05 flight?
Could she take an express train?

information questions

Which trains **could** I take?
Who can give me the information?
When should they leave?

A Complete each sentence or question.

1. Who _____ the tickets?
should buy / should to buy

2. Where _____ a hotel?
I can find / can I find

3. You _____ or _____ the bus.
could to walk / could walk   take / taking

4. _____ you when I arrive?
I should call / Should I call

5. We _____ the bus; it left five minutes ago.
can to not take / can't take

6. When _____ the agent your boarding pass?
should you giving / should you give

7. Which trains _____ me there before dinnertime?
can get / can getting

UNIT 9 Lesson 2

Expression of future actions

There are four ways to express future actions using the present tenses. These are similar in meaning.

be going to

be going to + base form usually expresses a future plan or certain knowledge about the future.

I'm going to spend my summer in Africa.   **She's going to get** a rental car when she arrives.
It's going to rain tomorrow.

The present continuous

The present continuous can also express a future plan.

We're traveling tonight.   They **aren't wearing** formal clothes to the wedding.
We aren't eating home tomorrow.

The simple present tense

The simple present tense can express a future action, almost always with verbs of motion: arrive, come, depart, fly, go, head, leave, sail, and start, especially when on a schedule or timetable. When the simple present tense expresses the future, there is almost always a word, phrase, or clause indicating the future time.

This Monday the express **leaves** at noon.

The present tense of be

The present tense of be can describe a future event if it includes a word or phrase that indicates the future.

The wedding **is on Sunday.**

Answer the following questions.

1. What are your plans for the summer?

   _____

2. What are you going to do this weekend?

   _____

3. What are you doing this evening?

   _____

B **Read the arrival and departure schedules. Then complete each question or statement with the simple present tense.**

TOMORROW'S BUS TO NEW YORK CITY

DEPARTURE	ARRIVAL
8:00	11:00

THURSDAY'S FLIGHT TO
GUATEMALA CITY

DEPARTURE / ARRIVAL
23:30   01:30

THIS WEEKEND'S TRAIN
TO BEIJING

DEPARTURE	ARRIVAL
07:00	22:20

1. The bus _____ at 11:00. It _____ at 8:00.
2. When _____ the flight _____? At 1:30.
3. The flight _____ at 23:30.
4. What time _____ the train _____ in Beijing? At ten-twenty at night.
5. _____ the train _____ at seven? Yes, it does.

UNIT 10 Lesson 1

┌─ **Comparison with adjectives** ─────────────────────

Comparative adjectives compare two people, places, or things.

    Mexico City is **bigger than** Los Angeles.

Superlative adjectives compare more than two people, places, or things.

    Mexico City is **the biggest** city in the Americas. (compared to all the other cities in the Americas)

adjective	comparative adjective	superlative adjective
cheap	**cheaper (than)**	**the cheapest**
expensive	**more expensive (than)**	**the most expensive**

┌─ **Superlative adjectives: form** ─────────────────────

Add _–est_ to one-syllable adjectives. If the adjective ends in _–e_, add _–st_. Remember to use _the_ with superlatives.

    cheap → **the** cheap**est**   loose → **the** loose**st**

If an adjective ends with consonant-vowel-consonant, double the final consonant before adding _–est_.

    hot → the ho**tt**est

For most adjectives that end in _–y_, change the _y_ to _i_ and add _–est_.

    pretty → the prett**iest**   busy → the bus**iest**

To make the superlative form of most adjectives of two or more syllables, use _the most_ or _the least_.

    Car trips are **the least relaxing** vacations.   Safaris are **the most exciting** vacations.

A Write the comparative and superlative form of the following adjectives.

	comparative	superlative		comparative	superlative
1. tall	_____	_____	**9.** informal	_____	_____
2. easy	_____	_____	**10.** interesting	_____	_____
3. liberal	_____	_____	**11.** conservative	_____	_____
4. heavy	_____	_____	**12.** light	_____	_____
5. unusual	_____	_____	**13.** casual	_____	_____
6. pretty	_____	_____	**14.** comfortable	_____	_____
7. exciting	_____	_____	**15.** relaxing	_____	_____
8. wild	_____	_____			

B Complete each sentence with a comparative or superlative adjective.

1. That dinner was _____ meal on our vacation.
delicious

2. This scanner is definitely _____ than that one.
good

3. The Caribbean cruise is _____ of our vacation packages.
relaxing

4. The Honshu X24 is a good camera, but the Cashio Speedo 5 is _____ to use.
easy

5. We have several brands, but I'd say the R300 is _____ .
popular

6. Sunday is going to be _____ day of the week. It's the end of my vacation!
bad

7. I like that vase, but I think this one is _____ .
beautiful

8. The Italian bowl was a good deal, but the Portuguese one was _____ .
nice

C Complete the conversations with a superlative adjective.

1. A: Well, we've got several brands to choose from.

  B: Which one's _____ ?
  good

2. A: Would you like to see these scanners?

  B: Sure. But which one's _____ to use?
  easy

3. A: I'm looking for a PDA. Which brand is _____ ?
  light

  B: Oh, that would be the Delio P500.

4. A: How much can you spend?

  B: Not too much. Which is _____ ?
  expensive

5. A: I love these plates. They're so unusual. Should we buy one?

  B: Sure. Which one do you think is _____ ?
  attractive

🎧 TOP NOTCH POP LYRICS

Going Out [Unit 2]

Do you want to see a play?
What time does the play begin?
It starts at eight.   Is that OK?
I'd love to go.   I'll see you then.
I heard it got some good reviews.
Where's it playing?   What's the show?
It's called "One Single Life to Lose."
I'll think about it.   I don't know.

(CHORUS)
Everything will be all right
when you and I go out tonight.

When Thomas Soben gives his talk—
The famous chef?   That's not for me!
The doors open at nine o'clock.
There's a movie we could see
at Smith and Second Avenue.
That's my favorite neighborhood!
I can't wait to be with you.
I can't wait to have some food.

(CHORUS)

We're going to have a good time.
Don't keep me up past my bedtime.
We'll make a date.
Tonight's the night.
It starts at eight.
The price is right!
I'm a fan of rock and roll.
Classical is more my style.
I like blues and I like soul.
Bach and Mozart make me smile!
Around the corner and down the street.
That's the entrance to the park.
There's a place where we could meet.
I wouldn't go there after dark!

(CHORUS: 2 times)

The World Café [Unit 5]

Is there something that you want?
Is there anything you need?
Have you made up your mind
what you want to eat?
Place your order now,
or do you need more time?
Why not start with some juice—
lemon, orange, or lime?
Some like it hot, some like it sweet,
some like it really spicy.
You may not like everything you eat,
but I think we're doing nicely.

(CHORUS)
I can understand every word you say.
Tonight we're speaking English at The
World Café.

I'll take the main course now.
I think I'll have the fish.
Does it come with a choice of another
   dish?
Excuse me waiter, please—
I think I'm in the mood
for a little dessert, and the cake looks good.

Do you know?   Are there any low-fat
desserts that we could try now?
I feel like having a bowl of fruit.
Do you have to say good-bye now?

(CHORUS)

Apples, oranges, cheese and ham,
coffee, juice, milk, bread, and jam,
rice and beans, meat and potatoes,
eggs and ice cream,
grilled tomatoes—
That's the menu.
That's the list.
Is there anything I missed?

(CHORUS)

A Typical Day [Unit 6]

The Couch Potato sits around.
He eats junk food by the pound.
It's just a typical day.
Watching as the world goes by,
he's out of shape and wonders why.
It's just a typical day.

(CHORUS)
Every night he dreams that he's
skydiving through the air.
And sometimes you appear.
He says, "What are you doing here?"

He cleans the house and plays guitar,
takes a shower, drives the car.
It's just a typical day.
He watches TV all alone,
reads and sleeps, talks on the phone.
It's just a typical day.

(CHORUS)

I'm sorry.
Mr. Couch Potato's resting right now.
Can he call you back?
He usually lies down every day of the week,
and he always has to have a snack.
Now all his dreams are coming true.
He's making plans to be with you.
It's just a typical day.
He goes dancing once a week.
He's at the theater as we speak!
It's just a typical day.

(CHORUS)

My Dream Vacation [Unit 8]

The ride was bumpy
and much too long.
It was pretty boring.
It felt so wrong.
I slept all night,
and it rained all day.
We left the road,
and we lost the way.
Then you came along
and you took my hand.
You whispered words
I could understand.

(CHORUS)
On my dream vacation,
I dream of you.

I don't ever want to wake up.
On my dream vacation,
this much is true:
I don't ever want it to stop.

The food was awful.
They stole my purse.
The whole two weeks went
from bad to worse.
They canceled my ticket.
I missed my flight.
They were so unfriendly
it just wasn't right.
So I called a taxi,
and I got inside,
and there you were,
sitting by my side.

(CHORUS)

You were so unusual.
The day was so exciting.
I opened up my eyes,
and you were gone.
I waited for hours.
You never called.
I watched TV
and looked at the walls.
Where did you go to?
Why weren't you near?
Did you have a reason
to disappear?
So I flew a plane
to the south of France,
and I heard you say,
"Would you like to dance?"

(CHORUS)

Shopping for Souvenirs [Unit 10]

I go to the bank at a quarter to ten.
I pick up my cash from the ATM.
Here at the store, it won't be too hard
to take out a check or a credit card.
The bank has a good rate of exchange,
and everything here is in my price range.
The easiest part of this bargain hunt
is that I can afford anything I want.

(CHORUS)
Whenever I travel around the world,
I spend my money for two.
Shopping for souvenirs
helps me to be near you.

I try to decide how much I should pay
for the beautiful art I see on display.
To get a great deal, I can't be too nice.
It can't hurt to ask for a better price.

(CHORUS)

Yes, it's gorgeous, and I love it.
It's the biggest and the best,
though it might not be the cheapest.
How much is it—more than all the rest?
I'll pass on some good advice to you:
When you're in Rome, do as the Romans do.
A ten percent tip for the taxi fare
should be good enough when you're staying
   there.

(CHORUS)

Intensifiers too, really, and very

Intensifiers make the meaning of adjectives stronger.

Too expresses the idea of "more than enough." **Too** has a negative meaning.

These shoes are **too** expensive. I'm not going to buy them.   That movie is **too** scary. I don't want to see it.

Very and **really** don't have negative meaning.

These shoes are **very** expensive. I like them.   That movie is **really** scary. I'm going to love it.

A Complete each sentence with a phrase using **too**, **really**, or **very**.

1. Beach vacations are _really relaxing_. I love them.

2. French fries are _____. You shouldn't eat them every day.

3. A safari vacation is _____. I don't have enough money to go.

4. This movie is _____. I want to see it.

5. Our house is _____. I don't want to sell it.

6. English is _____. Many people study it.

7. This printer is _____. I need a new one.

8. Those pants are _____! You should wear something more conservative.

B Complete the conversations. Write the adjectives with **too** or **enough**.

1. **A:** How about this necklace? Should we buy it for your mother?

   B: No. It isn't _____. I want something nicer.
   pretty

2. **A:** Look. I bought this rug today. Do you think it's too small?

   B: No. I think it's _____.
   big

3. **A:** I'm sending this steak back to the chef.

   B: Why? What's wrong?

   A: It's just not _____.
   good

4. **A:** How was your vacation?

   B: Well, to tell the truth, it just wasn't _____.
   relaxing

5. **A:** Did you buy a microwave oven?

   B: I looked at some yesterday. But they were _____.
   expensive

6. **A:** You don't eat candy?

   B: No. It's _____ for me.
   sweet

7. **A:** How's that soup? Is it _____?
   hot
   B: No, it's fine. Thanks.

8. **A:** Do you want any ice in your water?

   B: No, thanks. It's _____.
   cold